UTAH

Michael R. Kelsey

MOUNTAINEERING

GUIDE And The Best Canyon Hikes

(63 maps and 88 fotos)

Kelsey Publishing Co.
310 East 950 South
Springville, Utah
USA   84663

First Edition February 1983

Library of Congress Catalog Card Number — 83-080147
ISBN Number 0-9605824-1-X

Climbers, hikers and travelers are requested to send corrections, comments, suggestions, and orders for books to the author at the following address:

Michael R. Kelsey
310 East 950 South
Springville, Utah, USA
84663   Tele. 801-489-6666

Printed by Press Publishing, Ltd.
            1601 West 800 North
            Provo, Utah 84601

All Fotos by the Author

All Maps, Charts, Diagrams, etc., Drawn by the Author

Cover Fotos

A. Lone Peak, East Face
B. Kings Peak from Henrys Fork Basin
C. Mt. Timpanogos from the North Ridge
D. Buckskin Gulch of the Paria River

TABLE OF CONTENTS

MAP SYMBOLS

Town or City . . . . ▫ ☐
Buildings or Homes . . . . ▫
Hut or Shelter . . . . △
Campgrounds . . . . ▲
Picnic Site . . . . ▲
Church . . . . ⚑
Ranger Station . . . . ♟
Guard Station . . . . 🏛
Ski lift or Tramway . . . . ⊢—⊣
Airport or Landing Strip . . . . ✈
Railway . . . . ┼┼┼┼
Interstate Highway . . . . 🛡70
U.S. Highway . . . . 🛡89
Utah State Highway . . . . ⬡12
Road-Unsurfaced . . . . ══
Road-4 Wheel Drive . . . . ≡≡≡
Trails . . . . ‒ ‒ ‒
Parking . . . . Ⓟ
Route, Climbing . . . . •••••
Peak . . . . ✖
Peak and Prominent Ridge . . . . ✖
River or Stream . . . . ∼
Narrows . . . . Ⓝ
River, Intermittent - Dry . . . . -·-·--
Lake . . . . ⬭
Mine, Quarry . . . . ⟍↗
Waterfalls . . . . ─╫─
Spring or Well . . . . ○
Spring, Intermittent . . . . Ⓢ
Glacier or Perpetual Snow . . . . ⬭⬭⬭
Undercut . . . .
Pass . . . . ≍
Natural Arch . . . . Ⓐ
Pictograph or Petrogylph . . . . Ⓟ
Steep Escarpment . . . . ─┬┬┬┬
Narrow Canyon . . . . ⟨⟨⟨⟨⟩⟩⟩⟩

ABBREVIATIONS

Canyon	C. or Can.	Picnic Ground	P.G.
Lake	L.	Reservoir	Res.
River	R.	Ranger Station	R.S.
Creek	CK.	Guard Station	G.S.
Campground	C.G.	4 Wheel Drive	4WD

Acknowledgments

It's impossible to recall at this time all the many people who have helped me put this book together. There are countless forest rangers who spent hours going over maps indicating trails or the lack of. Also the BLM rangers and national parks employees who made recommendations as to the best hikes, especially in the southeastern part of Utah. There was also other hikers and climbers who gave information.

But the one person who helped most, the one person who spent hours going over the maps and especially the manuscript, and the one person who just simply put up with me, was my mother, Venetta Kelsey.

The Author

The author experienced his earliest years of life in Eastern Utah's Uinta Basin, namely around the town of Roosevelt. Later the family moved to Provo, where he attended Provo High School, and later Brigham Young University, where he earned a B.S. degree in Sociology. Soon after he discovered that was the wrong subject, so he attended the University of Utah, where he received his Masters of Science degree in Geography, finishing that in June, 1970.

It was then that real life began, for on June 9, 1970, he put a pack on his back and started traveling for the first time. He has now (February 1983) been on the road on 14 different trips for a total of 86 months, and has seen about 100 countries. All this led the author to write and publish a book entitled, *"Climbers and Hikers Guide to the Worlds Mountains"*, published in 1981. At this time he is continuing to work on that book and is looking forward to the second edition coming out in the not too distant future.

After having climbed or attempted most of the mountains in the world guide, he then "settled down" to do what he has dreamed about for many years, a mountaineering guide to Utah.

The author and his father take a rest at Trail Rider Pass, not far from Lake Atwood, in the upper Uinta River drainage. The lower slopes of Mt. Emmons seen in the background (50mm lens).

INTRODUCTION

For the most part this book consists of maps of mountains and some canyons and hiking areas within the state of Utah. Each map is accompanied by a page of written information and one fotograph. The written part includes sections on location of mountains or hiking areas, geology, access routes and problems, trail information, time needed for the hike or climb, the best time of year for an outing in each location, and a list of forest service or U.S.G.S. maps available for each area.

All the hikes and climbs in this book are divided into 5 different regions. They include: The Great Basin, located in western Utah, extending from the Nevada border eastward to the Wasatch Mountains and the central Utah Plateaus. Next section is the Greater Wasatch Mountains. This includes all the mountains from Mt. Nebo in the south, north to the Idaho border, along the Wasatch Front. It also includes the Bear River and Wellsville Mountains near the Idaho line. After that is the part including peaks and summits on the High Plateaus of central and southern Utah. One of these ranges, the Canyon Range near Scipio, could be put in either the Great Basin or in with the High Plateaus. The fourth section is of the Uinta Mountains in the northeast part of the state. And the last part, covering all the area of southeastern Utah, is called the Canyonlands. It could also be called the Colorado Plateau. It includes five mountain areas and all of the canyon hikes in the book.

Each of these areas are interesting in their own way and each area has its own unique problems for travel or access, its own vegetation and to some degree its own climate. For example, in the Great Basin, distances are usually long and travel is always partly on gravel roads. However these roads are generally well maintained, and on many driving can be done at or near highway speeds. The Great Basin is also a dry area, so climbers and hikers should take extra amounts of water in the vehicle, as well as extra gasoline in some cases. In most other areas of the state, one can travel on paved roads to very near the intended hike or climb, with only a few exceptions, most of which are in the Canyonlands region. The Canyonlands region is another dry area, and water should always be carried in one;s vehicle. The Canyonlands part is another region having some stretches of long dusty roads. All other parts of the state are well watered and have only short lengths of gravel or dirt roads leading to mountains.

Other topics covered in this guide which are of interest to climbers and hikers, are the bristlecone pine trees located in the Great Basin part of Utah. Later on in this book is a map showing locations of this tree, both in Utah and the west. This tree is the oldest living thing on earth, and Utah has a fair number of peaks where the bristlecone pine is found.

Also found in another section of this book is a map showing peaks which were used in the 1880's as Heliograph or triangulation stations. These survey stations were set up on some of the highest and most prominent peaks as the U.S. Coast and Geodetic Survey crossed the state while surveying the USA along the 39th parallel. There is some evidence of these stations on most of the peaks indicated, and in some cases, stone walled houses are still standing. Ibapah and Belknap Peaks have the best ruins.

To help the reader become better acquainted with Utahs weather patterns, and especially those climbers from out-of-state and perhaps even foreign travelers, a group of climographs have been created which show the annual rainfall, elevation, annual temperature range, temperature curve, monthly precipitation and length of growing season, of 19 of Utahs cities and towns. These charts or climographs show in a graphic way the difference in the weather patterns throughout the state. And there are great differences in rainfall and temperature patterns from one part of the state to another, especially from north to south, and from near the Great Salt Lake to areas away from that lake.

To help the reader understand the processes which have formed the earth and especially those parts of Utah where hiking is of interest, a number of geologic cross sections have been drawn. Several are enlarged, but a number of others are included right on the maps of hiking areas. These smaller cross sections are on maps of the Canyonlands hikes. These cross sections show the different beddings or formations, but not the age of the rock. In many cases they also show Anazasi ruins in relation to overhangs and the sun, and natural bridges. The climber or hiker should find these geologic cross sections both interesting and informative.

Another chart or list in the back of the book compares the highest peaks in the state. There are 12 summits in Utah over 4000 meters (13123 feet), all of which are found in the Uinta Mountains of the northeast. There's another list of peaks over 3600 meters (11810 feet). This is for all peaks outside the Uinta Mountains, namely in the La Sal, the Tushar, and the Deep Creek Ranges. Mt. Timpanogos isn't even in this group, as it's only 3582 meters. All elevations in this book are in meters and all distances are in kilometers. So for the reader who doesn't yet comprehend metrics, there's a chart or conversion table in the book as well.

In several of the canyon hikes covered in this book, mention is made of the ruins and rock art in those areas. So a map and a short piece of information has been prepared shedding light on the Anasazi and Fremont Indian ruins and pictographs and petroglyphs. Nowhere else can one view *outdoor museums,* such as those found in the southeastern corner of Utah.

Also included in the back of this book is a list of BLM (Bureau of Land Management) offices, forest service ranger stations, national parks and park office headquarters, and the locations of places where maps can be found and purchased. Included is an index map showing the states new 1:100,000 scale maps (metric).

This book differs from a lot of other guide books in that there is no advice as to how to climb mountains, or how to get on in the wilderness. It's assumed that the reader will already know most of the basics before getting involved with real mountaineering, or before he or she gets too far into some of the long canyon hikes. But here are some tips concerning equipment. For the Uinta Mountains a good tent with rainsheet is the one most important piece of equipment to be taken. Also, a raincoat or piece of plastic for the hiker is needed because of the frequency of summer showers. In early summer mesquito repellent is a must — again in the Uintas. When hiking in the canyons, which arevery dry regions, one can usually get by without a tent, but it's always a more comfortable camp if one is inside away from the insects. The author takes and uses a tent no matter where he's hiking or climbing. Footwear is almost exclusively the leather hiking or climbing boot, either medium or high top. But for the canyon hikes the recently introduced rubber, leather and nylon walking or hiking shoe seems ideal. Up till now the jungle boots have been the most popular footwear used in the canyons, along with the common running shoe. The reason for the change of footwear in the canyons is that in most cases there are no trails and one simply walks in the sandy canyon bottom, and many times in the stream itself.

For those hiking in the canyons of southeastern Utah, water is sometimes a problem. Actually, there's plenty around, but you'll have to know where it is, and plan your campsites accordingly. Before entering any of the canyons mentioned in this book, always stop at the park visitor center, or the nearest BLM office or ranger station, for the latest word on the availability of water and its whereabouts. Be prepared by taking extra water bottles in your car and in your pack. By having the potential to carry water, finding a campsite is made easier, especially if time is a factor.

A hat is an important piece of equipment, although most don't use one. The author has been climbing and hiking around the world for 13 years without a hat, and now is afflicted with "sun spots"; that's stage one on the road to skin cancer. Utah is generally a dry state with lots of sunshine, so the use of a hat or cap of some kind is important.

One should think about the use of a small climbers or backpackers stove. As time goes on, and as climbing and hiking become more popular, some popular camping spots will become wood scarce. This is especially true around some lakes in the High Uintas, in the central Wasatch Mountains, and a few sites in some canyons in the southeast part of the state. The author carries the smallest kerosene stove available in his pack at all times and it is an indispensable part of his camping gear. The new stoves these days weigh almost nothing and take up a very small space in one's pack.

Some writers spend a lot of time lecturing about leaving a clean campsite, carrying out all trash, leaving all ruins undistrubed, not cutting pine boughs for bedding, etc., etc. This book does not, beyond this line. The author has found that people reading books such as this one are almost always considerate of nature and of those who will follow. It appears to be someone else, people who will never see, or least of all, read this book, who are leaving their beer and soda pop cans all about for posterity to view. Since they won't be reading this book there'll be no further mention of the above topics.

The author has spent years hiking and climbing in the state, years dreaming of putting together this book and a couple of years in direct preparation in writing and publishing this book and now hopes each reader can have even more enjoyable moments than the author as a result of the information and maps presented here.

METRIC CONVERSION TABLE

1 Centimeter = .39 Inch
1 Inch = = 2.54 Centimeters
1 Meter = 39.37 Inches
1 Foot = 0.3048 Meter
1 Kilometer = 0.621 Mile
1 Mile = 1.609 Kilometers
100 Miles = 161 Kilometers
100 Kilometers = 62 Miles

1 Liter = 1.101 Quarts
1 Quart = .908 Liter
1 Gallon (US) = 3.63 Liters
1 Acre = 0.405 Hector
1 Hector = 2.471 Acres

METERS TO FEET (Meters × 3.2808 = Feet)
(WELL-KNOWN PLACES AND MOUNTAINS)

100 m = 328 ft. .... Bakersfield, California—128 m
500 m = 1640 ft. ...... Mt. Christoffel, Curacao, Caribbean—370 m
1000 m = 3281 ft. ...... St. George, Utah—878 m
1500 m = 4921 ft. ...... Tooele, Utah—1539 m
2000 m = 6562 ft. ...... Aspen Grove, Mt. Timpanogos—2089 m
2500 m = 8202 ft. ...... Snowbird Resort, Utah—2500 m
3000 m = 9842 ft. ...... Ben Lomond Peak, Utah—2961 m
3500 m = 11483 ft. ..... Mt. Timpanogos, Utah—3582 m
4000 m = 13124 ft. ....., Kings Peak, Utah—4123 m
4500 m = 14764 ft. ..... Mt. Whitney, California, 4419 m
5000 m = 16404 ft. ..... Mt. Stanley, Uganda—5119 m
5500 m = 18044 ft. ..... Damavand, Iran—5671 m
6000 m = 19686 ft. ..... Kilimanjaro, Tanzania—5963 m
6500 m = 21325 ft. ..... Illimani, Bolivia—6402 m
7000 m = 22966 ft. ..... Aconcagua, Argentina—6959 m
7500 m = 24606 ft. ..... Minya Konka, China—7589 m
8000 m = 26246 ft. ..... Annapurna, Nepal—8078 m
8500 m = 27887 ft. ..... Kangchenjunga, Nepal-Sikkim—8598 m
9000 m = 29527 ft. ..... Mt. Everest, Nepal-China—8848 m

FEET TO METERS (Feet ÷ 3.2808 = Meters)

1000 ft. = 305 m	16000 ft. = 4877 m
2000 ft. = 610 m	17000 ft. = 5182 m
3000 ft. = 914 m	18000 ft. = 5486 m
4000 ft. = 1219 m	19000 ft. = 5791 m
5000 ft. = 1524 m	20000 ft. = 6096 m
6000 ft. = 1829 m	21000 ft. = 6401 m
7000 ft. = 2134 m	22000 ft. = 6706 m
8000 ft. = 2438 m	23000 ft. = 7010 m
9000 ft. = 2743 m	24000 ft. = 7315 m
10000 ft. = 3048 m	25000 ft. = 7620 m
11000 ft. = 3353 m	26000 ft. = 7925 m
12000 ft. = 3658 m	27000 ft. = 8230 m
13000 ft. = 3962 m	28000 ft. = 8535 m
14000 ft. = 4268 m	29000 ft. = 8839 m
15000 ft. = 4572 m	30000 ft. = 9144 m

REFERENCE MAP

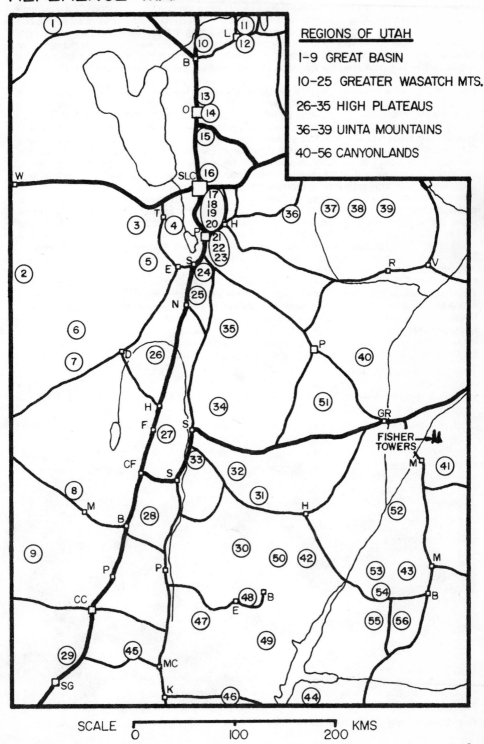

REGIONS OF UTAH

1-9 GREAT BASIN

10-25 GREATER WASATCH MTS.

26-35 HIGH PLATEAUS

36-39 UINTA MOUNTAINS

40-56 CANYONLANDS

FISHER TOWERS

SCALE

0   100   200   KMS

1. Bull Mountain, Raft River Mountains

Location One of the least known ranges in the state of Utah is the Raft River Mountains in the extreme northwest corner of the state. The range runs east-west, a rare thing in the USA. The highest peak is Bull Mountain, at 3028 meters. It's merely the high point on a long, flat and undulating ridge. The local economy is based on the raising of sheep, cattle, jackrabbits, alfalfa and wheat, and the mining of building stone, namely the green-colored rock, olivine. The northern half of the range is under the control of the Sawtooth National Forest, while the southern parts are managed by the Hereford Association out of Park Valley.

Geology The same forces which made the Uintas also made the Raft Rivers. The mountain core is quartzite, with intrusive bodies on both the north and south slopes (granite).

Access One should drive to Snowville on I-84, then drive west on US Highway 42-30. Proceed to Strevel, Clear Creek and to the Clear Creek Campground — if the all-public-land access route is desired. This route has about 16 kms of dusty, but well-maintained roads (Strevel to Clear Creek Campground). The easiest approach is via Park Valley, but the land between the highway and the mountains is private. This is usually no problem though, simply ask a local rancher for permission to cross the associations land. At the church in Park Valley, turn north and follow the main road to its end, go through a gate, then proceed to the mouth of Fisher Creek Canyon.

Trail Information There are no forest service maintained trails in the entire range. However, there are abundant cattle trails throughout all the canyons, especially on the southern slopes. Along the summit ridge, which is open and grassy, there's a 4WD road. One can reach this summit ridge via Left Hand Fork of Dunn Creek or Fisher Creek on the south, or from Clear Creek Campground and Lake Fork Creek on the north. The canyons are wooded, mostly with douglas fir — the ridges are open and grassy. The best area for rock climbers is in the cirque basin holding Bull Lake. The canyons are all well watered. Some streams even have fish.

Best Time and Time Needed From Salt Lake City it's a 3-4 hour drive to the Raft River Mountains. Then hikers can reach the higher summits from the north or the south in one day, which means a two day outing for the average hiker. These mountains receive heavy winter snows but little summer rain, therefore mid-June through October are the normal months for hiking.

Campgrounds Clear Creek C.G. is on public land, as is most of the north slope.

Maps Utah Travel Council Map 8 — Northwestern Utah, Sawtooth National Forest, U.S.G.S. maps Grouse Creek (1:100,000), Yost, Park Valley, Kelton Pass (1:62,500)

From Summit Ridge of Raft Rivers, looking east over Bull Lake and cirque basin (17mm lens).

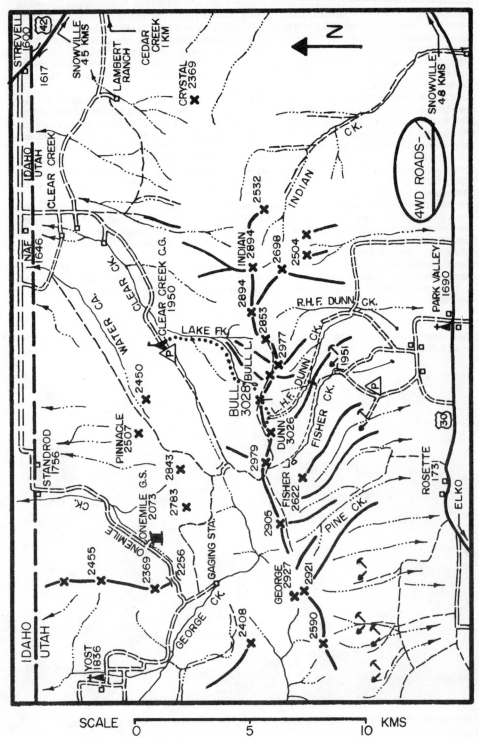

SCALE

0   5   10   KMS

2. Ibapah Peak, Deep Creek Range

Location The Deep Creek Range, in which Ibapah Peak at 3684 meters is the highest summit, is located in extreme western Utah and about 100 kms south of Wendover. This range is part of the Basin and Range System of mountains which covers all of Nevada and parts of Utah. The Goshute Indian Reservation is located on the western slopes and the range is under the control of the BLM. On top of Ibapah Peak are the remains of an old Heliograph Station dating from the early 1880's.

Geology The north and south ends of the Deep Creeks is made of Precambrian rock, quartzite. But the central core including the highest peaks is composed of a Tertiary intrusive body of granite. The area is pocked with old mines.

Access For Utahns, this is one of the more isolated ranges in the state. The best approach is via Interstate 80 to Wendover, then south on US Highway 93, and finally east to Ibapah and Callao. One can also reach the east side of the range via Dugway or Vernon, and the old stage coach line running to Fish Springs. One can climb on the west side of the range, but most of the better camping spots and most running water seems to be on the eastern slope. The author climbed the peaks via Indian Farm Creek, but it's likely the route up Granite Creek is the better and most direct route to Ibapah Peak. A third access route is from the Delta area and Highway 50-6. From near the Utah-Nevada line, drive north to Gandy, then Trout Creek. Ibapah is the only settlement in the area that has food and gasoline available. Be prepared for long, dusty rides.

Trail Information Because of its isolation, there are very few people visiting the Deep Creeks — as a result, there are few if any trails. There are some 4WD roads to most of the canyon mouths, but beyond those points, one must usually route-find. There's a cattle trail going over the pass between Ibapah and Red Mountain. If this trail is taken, simply walk from the pass to the summit. Water exists in most of the canyons, but flows no further than the canyon mouths.

Best Time and Time Needed It will take most of one day for people in Utah to reach these mountains. From somewhere on Granite Creek it will take one day for the actual hike, then perhaps another day for the return trip. But a fast hiker and driver can make the entire trip from say Salt Lake, in two long days. Climbing season, late June through October.

Campgrounds No BLM campgrounds here, but good campsites exist in the mouths of all major canyons on the east slope.

Maps Utah Travel Council Map 7 — Northwestern Central Utah, U.S.G.S. maps Fish Springs (1:100,000), Trout Creek (1:62,500), Ibapah Peak, Indian Farm Creek, Goshute, Goshute Canyon (1:24,000)

From summit of Ibapah, one can see the second highest peak, Haystack Mt. (50mm lens).

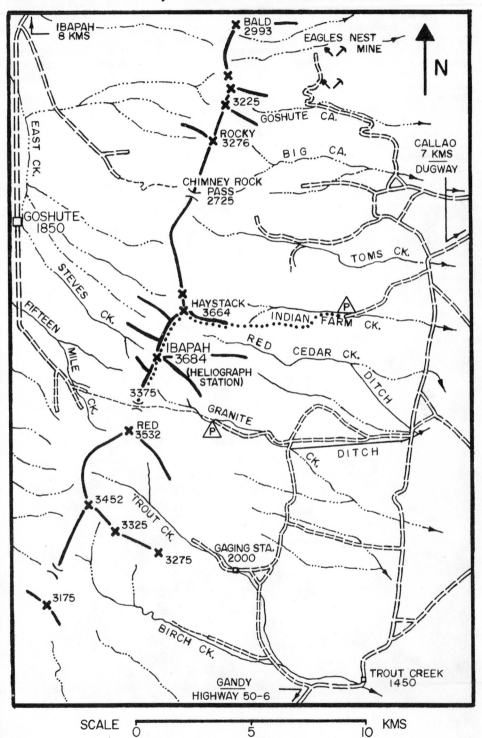

SCALE 0 ___ 5 ___ 10 KMS

3. Deseret Peak, Stansbury Range

Location The Stansbury Range is located in Tooele County about 25 kms due west of the town of Tooele, and about 70 kms west of Salt Lake City. The highest peak in the range is Deseret Peak, rising to 3363 meters. These mountains are almost unknown outside Tooele County, but they have several fine peaks and some nice hiking trails. There's even catchable fish in South Willow Creek.

Geology The geology of the Stansbury Range is similar to that of other Great Basin mountains. The earth's crustal folding has exposed the Oquirrh Formation, mostly limestone, on the eastern slopes, but the highest peaks are composed mostly of the Tintic Quartzite. Cirque basins indicate these peaks were heavily glaciated in the past.

Access The single most important access road is the one running south out of Grantsville. Follow the signs into the South Willow Creek drainage. From Grantsville to the end of the road is about 20 kms, of which about 13 are paved. By parking at the upper end of the Loop Campground, one can reach all parts of the range via the trail leaving that point. Another route of access would be North Willow Creek, and East Hickman Canyon, but the roads into these canyons are less well-maintained.

Trail Information The trails in the Stansbury Range are well-maintained and moderately used. The most used trail is the one running to the top of Deseret Peak. It begins at the end of the road in South Willow Canyon. At the first junction, a sign points the way up Mill Fork and to the top. This trail fades somewhat as it reaches the eastern summit ridge, but at that point the way is easy to find. Once on top you'll have a choice of descent routes. You may return the same way, or better still, return via the trail following the north ridge. This trail eventually joins the main trail running from North to South Willow Creeks. There's plenty of water in the canyons, but on the higher ridges there is none. The vegetation is similar to that in the Wasatch Mountains. The northeastern face of Deseret Peak has some fine rock climbing routes.

Best Time and Time Needed From Loop Campgrounds it's about 7 kms to the top of Deseret Peak, with a rise of about 1000 meters. Fast hikers can do it in a couple of hours, but for most hikers it'll be a half-day hike. From Salt Lake, an all day trip. Mid-June on through October is the hiking season. Because of the elevation of Deseret Peak, precipitation is very similar to that along the Wasatch Mountains.

Campgrounds Campgrounds are small and uncrowded, except on weekends. All forest service campgrounds are in South Willow Canyon, along with a guard station.

Maps Utah Travel Council Map 7 — Northwestern Central Utah, Wasatch-Cache National Forest, U.S.G.S. maps Tooele, Rush Valley (1:100,000), Timpie, Deseret Peak (1:62,500)

Deseret Peak in the Stansbury Range, showing the northeast face (35mm lens).

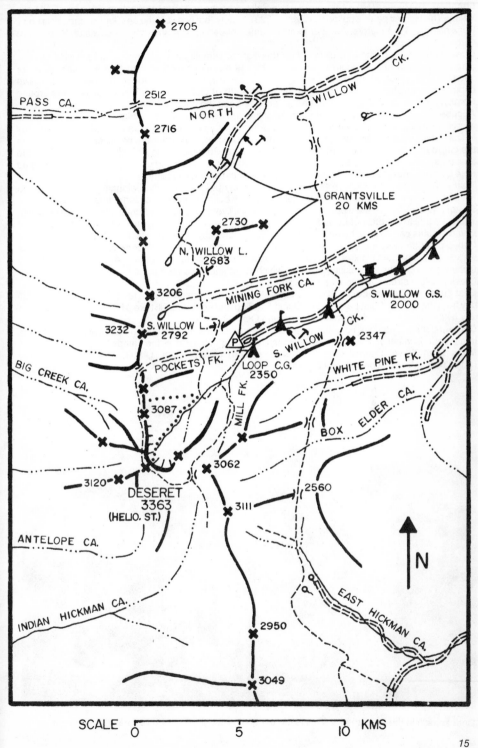

SCALE

0   5   10   KMS

4. Lowe Peak, Oquirrh Mountains

Location The Oquirrh Mountains are west of Salt Lake City, and form the western side of the Salt Lake Valley. The highest peak is called Flat Top, at 3237 meters, but possibly the best known summit is Lowe Peak rising to 3228 meters. Another familiar name appearing on many maps is Lewiston Peak, 3173 meters.

Geology If you're hiking and climbing on the highest summits in this range, you'll be walking over different portions of the Oquirrh Formation. This is mostly limestone, with layers of sandstone or quartzite. But notice all the mining symbols in the southwestern part of the map. There are intrusive bodies forming Sharp, Bald, and Dry Peaks just north of Ophir, and another intrusive body around Porphyry Hill north of Mercur. Gold and silver have been the primary metals mined here.

Access The route used by the author in reaching and climbing Lewiston, Flat Top and Lowe Peaks, was Highway 73 running between Tooele and Lehi. From this well-traveled road one can drive the 5 kms to Ophir, then on dirt roads to Ophir and South Fork Canyons. The northern peaks can be reached via the dirt road running between Riverton and Tooele, up Butterfield Canyon. Also, one can get to the eastern side by leaving Highway 73 just north of Cedar Fort and driving up West Canyon. The road up Pole Canyon from Cedar Fort would make southern peaks easy to climb.

Trail Information The Oquirrh Mountains are entirely private property, belonging mostly to mining interests and are not a part of any national forest. However, getting to the higher peaks is no problem. Sheep and cattle graze the slopes in summer, thus it's livestock and deer hunter's trails you'll be using. There's a trail to the base of Lowe from the end of the road in Ophir Canyon. Once at the base, one of several routes can then be taken. One may or may not be able to get a vehicle up South Fork of Ophir Canyon, but an easy route can be found up the west ridge of Lewiston, or an old 4WD road can be walked to a cabin just west of Flat Top, then up the west ridge to the summit. An advantage of using Ophir Canyon, is the availability of water, which is lacking in some other canyons mentioned. Ophir Creek is a fine stream above where it is piped out.

Best Time and Time Needed Climbing Lowe Peak is an easy half-day hike for many, but will take a full day from the Provo or Salt Lake Areas. Doing Flat Top and Lewiston will take a bit longer, but still a one day hike. Hiking season is from June 1 through October.

Campgrounds There are no constructed campgrounds here, but one can camp anyplace. Most of the larger springs in canyon bottoms have access roads, so these make fine campsites.

Maps Utah Travel Council Map 7 — Northwestern Central Utah, U.S.G.S. maps Rush Valley (1:100,000), Mercur, Lowe Peak (1:24,000)

Deer season in the Oquirrh Mts. This is the dry southwest slopes of Lowe Peak (35mm lens).

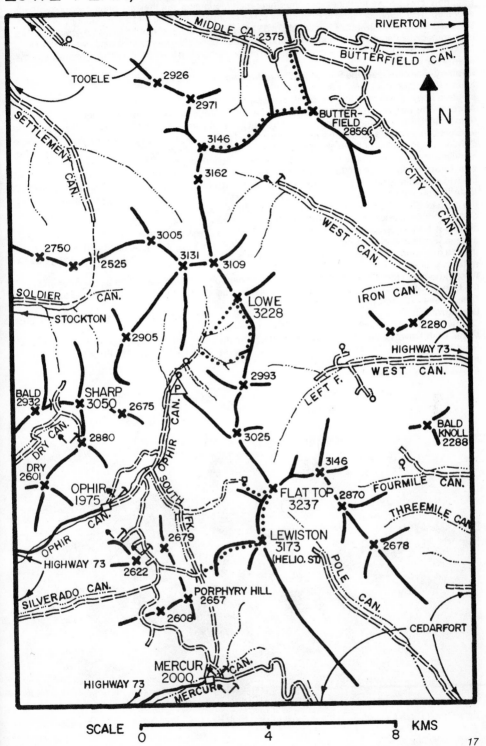

5. Black Crook Peak, Sheeprock Mountains

Location Few people have heard of the Sheeprock Mountains, but they are practically on our back door step. This compact range is located just to the south and southwest of the community of Vernon. Vernon is situated northwest of Eureka about 35 kms, and 56 kms south of Tooele on Highway 36. The land immediately south of Vernon is flat and has been used as experimental pastures by the Uinta National Forest. On the map are numerous 4WD roads extending from the Benmore Pastures into the nearby canyons.

Geology The geology of the Sheeprock Range is complex, but the exposed rock on the higher peaks is mostly Precambrian in age, with quartzite the dominant rock type. (Big Cottonwood Formation). An intrusive body is evident on the south slopes where all the old mines are shown.

Access The only logical approach to the Sheeprock Range is via Vernon and Highway 36. From Vernon drive west on Sharp Road towards Lookout Pass, but turn south on Harker Road. Drive south to where the fenced area terminates, then turn west and southwest heading in the direction of North Pine Canyon just to the left of the highest peak, Black Crook at 2827 meters. There's a good spring in the canyon and many cow trails. This is the best access route to the highest summits.

Trail Information There are few if any trails as such in the Sheeprock Mountains. In the past there has been mining activity here and as a result many roads and trails once existed. But today it's necessary to route-find up to the higher peaks. In most cases it's easier to climb a ridge, but that's not always true. In the case of Black Crook Peak, the best route might be to walk up the right-hand fork of North Pine Canyon beginning not far above the spring and water trough. This involves some bushwhacking. To climb Dutch Peak, 2733 meters, drive or walk up Bennion Creek to some of the old mines, then to the summit. For Pole and Mine Peaks, drive southwest above the Little Valley Campground. Keep in mind this is a dry mountain range. The only running water is in Little Valley and Vernon Creeks. Always carry water in your vehicle.

Best Time and Time Needed The amount of time needed for hiking any of these peaks depends on the type of vehicle one has. With a 4WD, any hike can be done easily in half a day, round trip. Hiking season here is from mid-May through about mid-November.

Campgrounds The only forest service campsite in the range is the Little Valley Campground. But one can camp anywhere. Best campsites are usually around springs.

Maps Utah Travel Council Map 7 — Northwestern Central Utah, Uinta National Forest, U.S.G.S. maps Rush Valley, Lynndyl (1:100,000), Lookout Pass, Vernon, Erickson Knoll, Dutch Peak (1:24,000)

Black Crook Peak as seen from the summit of Red Pine Peak (105mm lens).

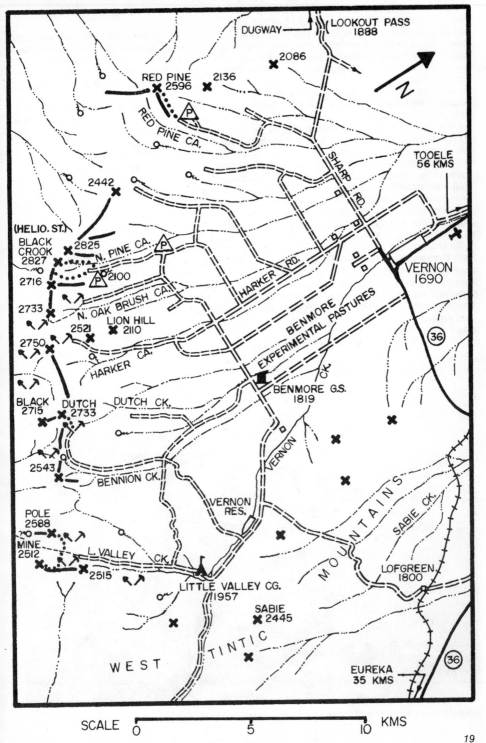

SCALE   0   5   10   KMS

6. Swasey Peak, House Range

Location The mountains on this map are in Utah's Great Basin. This is the House Range, about 60 kms due west of Delta and directly north of the Sevier Dry Lake Bed. The highest point on this map and the entire range is Swasey Peak at 2947 meters.

Geology The rocks in the northern part of the House Range are almost the same as those to the south around Notch Peak. It's almost all limestone. There's the Swasey Limestone, Marjum Formation and the Tatow Formation. The bedding is tilted to the east, with a fault line running along the western edge of the range. The result is a sharp and nearly vertical escarpment on the western edge of the peaks. Many parts of the escarpment rise from 100 to 200 vertical meters. On top of Swasey is a stand of bristlecone pines, a tree that does well on limestone soils.

Access There are many old roads in the valleys and mountains of the Great Basin, some of which are well-maintained. Some lead to present day mining activity, others are used by ranchers running cattle in the more favorable area. The main road to be used by most Utahns gaining access to Swasey Peak is the one beginning about 19 kms west of Delta and about 8 kms west of Hinckley. This well-used gravel road is well-marked. There's a signpost pointing the way to Antelope Spring and Marjum Pass. One could also reach Swasey Peak from the Notch Peak area. See Notch Peak map for more information. These valley roads can accommodate traffic at highway speeds.

Trail Information There are a few cattle trails in these mountains, but mostly it's 4WD roads. This means some bushwhacking is required to reach the summits of peaks. This is especially true of the southwest ridge of Swasey Peak. The brush there is very thick and difficult to penetrate. It's therefore recommended that one drive or walk along the road leading to the west face of Swasey, then route-find up a western ridge or face not far beyond Sinbad Spring (marked 2400). There is no live or running water in the entire range, so take note on the locations of springs which are usually piped to tanks.

Best Time and Time Needed The road beyond Antelope Spring is steep and rough, so for many that's the place to park. For those driving beyond it's a half-day hike to the summit of Swasey. But from the spring it may take a full day for many. Because of the low elevation and the resultant light amount of snowfall, Swasey can be climbed from May through November.

Campgrounds There are no maintained campgrounds in the House Range, but water has been piped from Antelope Spring down to the Trilobite Quarries with a water tap as shown.

Maps Utah Travel Council Map 6 — Southwestern Central Utah, U.S.G.S. maps Tule Valley (1:100,000), Marjum Pass, Swasey Peak (1:24,000)

Looking at the north end of the House Range, from the top of Swasey Peak (105mm lens).

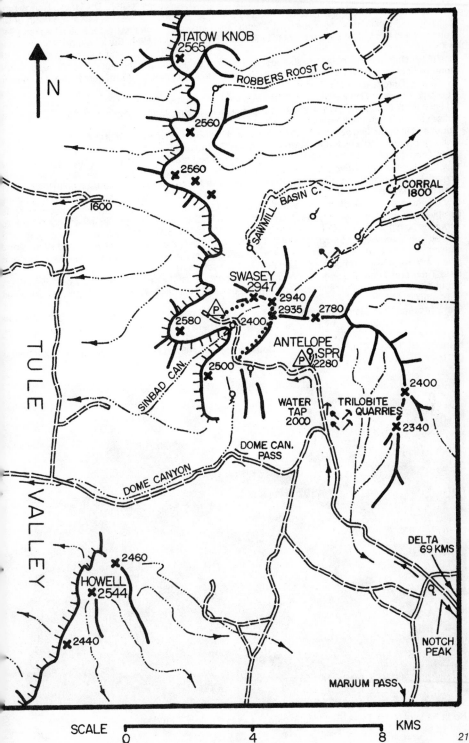

7. Notch Peak, House Range

Location The mountain range here is the House Range of west central Utah. The House Range run north-south in Utah's Great Basin. More exactly it's about 60 kms due west of Delta and north of US Highway 50-6 which runs east-west across Utah. The highest peak on this map is Notch Peak at 294: meters. Notch Peak is perhaps the single best rock climbing peak in Utah. But it's almost unknown due to it's isolated position. The west face of the north-south ridge has a tremendous drop, with the north face of Notch Peak itself being the steepest and highest vertical drop in the state. There's nearly a 400 meter vertical drop on Notches north face, while there's a drop of nearly 1600 meters from the summit to the floor of Tule Valley just 5 kms away.

Geology The entire House Range has been uplifted and tilted slightly to the east. The entire mountain is Notch Peak Limestone, a thick and massive hulk of solid limestone. The mines in the area are at the bottom of the Notch Peak Formation.

Access If approaching from the Utah or east side of the range, drive west out of Delta about 67 kms to a well-signposted road which runs north to Antelope Spring and Swasey Peak. This is on US Highway 50-6. Then drive about 5 kms north on this well-maintained graveled road 'till a signpost points out the way to Miller Canyon. Drive this road to the stone cabin as shown. The road to Swasey Peak is good enough to drive at highway speeds and the road to Miller Canyon is in good condition up to the cabin.

Trail Information There are no trails in this range, only a few 4WD type tracks leading into canyons and mining areas. Park at the stone cabin just mentioned, then walk up Sawtooth Canyon which is completely dry. Take all your water. It's walking on a 4WD track at first, then in the dry creek bed. At about the point the 4WD track fades, turn left into the left fork of Sawtooth Canyon. This is only about 3 kms up from the cabin. Once in this canyon it's a straight shot to the summit in a narrow and steep-sided canyon. No difficulties are found on this route. Just east of the summit are two groves of bristlecone pines. Interested rock climbers could try the west canyon route.

Best Time and Time Needed This normal route could be used as early as late April or May, and on through November. Strong climbers can climb the normal route easily in half a day, but most parties will want a full day.

Campgrounds No campground here, but if taking in Swasey Peak in the same trip, camp at Antelope Spring, shown on the Swasey Peak map. Only water here is at Painter Spring — no running water anywhere near.

Maps Utah Travel Council Map 6 — Southwestern Central Utah, U.S.G.S. maps Tule Valley (1:100,000), Notch Peak (1:62,500)

North Face of Notch Peak. Bristlecone pines seen in the upper left (35mm lens).

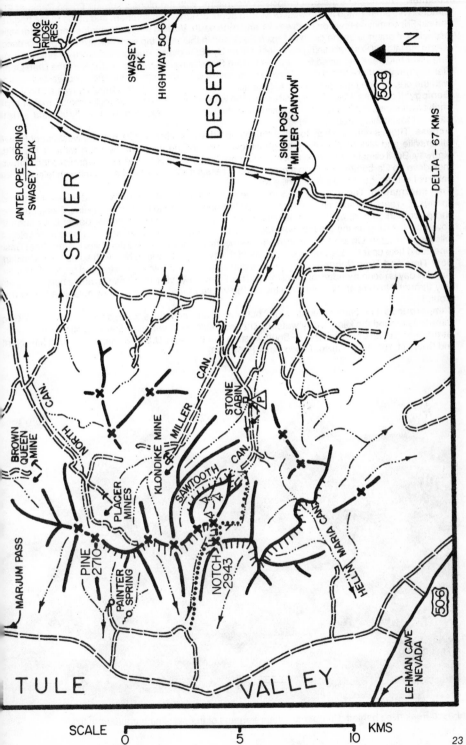

8. Frisco Peak, San Francisco Mountains

Location This range is the San Francisco Mountains, with the highest summit Frisco Peak, at 29- meters. This small range is due west of Milford about 30 kms. The southern end of the range begins the old Frisco mining town on Highway 21 and runs north. Visiting these mountains can be interestin especially if one makes the climb to Frisco Peak and in the same trip visits the remains of old Frisco. was in the late 1800's that mining was most active. By 1885, over 60 million $US worth of zinc, lead, go and silver had been extracted from the Rich Horn Silver Mine. There was a branch of the Utah Centr Railway running there (the old grade can still be seen) which brought water and supplies and returne with the ore. At one time there were 4000 inhabitants living there. By the 1920's it was a ghost tow

Geology If climbing Frisco Peak itself one will be walking over Precambrian rocks, mostly metamorph such as quartzite. But in areas of this map which show the old mines, an intrusive body is found, as is th case in most mining areas.

Access There's only one way to reach Frisco and that's on Highway 21 running west out of Beave Minersville and Milford. If visiting the ghost town most of the ruins can be seen within 1 km of th highway. But if climbing the peak, one must turn north where the old railway grade crosses the highwa' then drive up Carbonate Gulch on a rough road. There's a 4WD road to the summit with telecommur cations facilities, but there's a nice hike too.

Trail Information There are no trails in these mountains, only 4WD roads to old mines and to mo: springs. To reach the summit on foot, drive up Carbonate Gulch to the two large kilns. Passenger car should be parked here as the way is very rough beyond. Then walk along the power lines, then th power cables lying on the ground, past Morehouse Spring and to the summit over a boulder field, st following the cable. On top one can witness bristlecone pines, and have a good view of the Great Basir One could hike up the ridge crestline from the highway but that's a long hike with some bushwhackinç

Best Time and Time Needed Strong hikers can walk from the kilns to the top and back in half a day but a full day is recommended for the climb and the Frisco town visit. Hikes can be made here from abou May through November. No running water in the whole range, so take your own. Only a few spring around.

Campgrounds No campgrounds here but there are countless campsites everywhere. Goo: campsites around the kilns. Carry water up the mountain — Morehouse Spring is often dry.

Maps Utah Travel Council Map 6 — Southwestern Central Utah, U.S.G.S. maps Wah Wah Mts. North and South (1:100,000), Frisco, Frisco Peak (1:62,500)

Frisco Peak rises behind a couple of kilns, remnants of the old mining era (35mm lens).

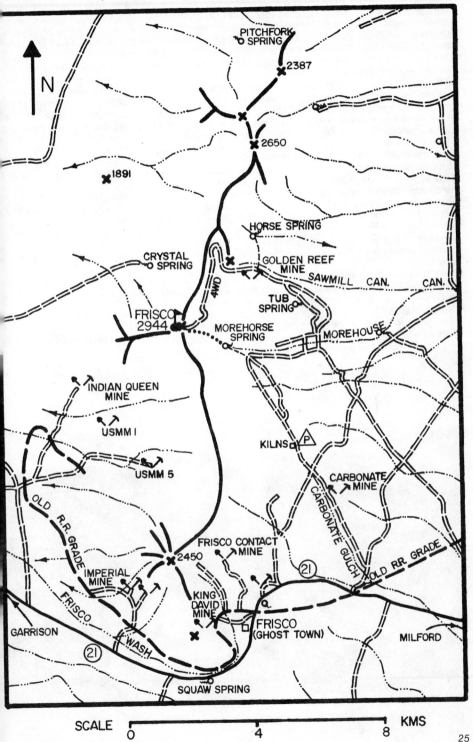

N

PITCHFORK SPRING

2387

2650

1891

HORSE SPRING

CRYSTAL SPRING

GOLDEN REEF MINE

SAWMILL CAN. CAN.

4WD

TUB SPRING

FRISCO 2944

MOREHORSE SPRING

MOREHOUSE

INDIAN QUEEN MINE

USMM 1

USMM 5

KILNS P

CARBONATE MINE

OLD R.R. GRADE

CARBONATE GULCH

OLD RR GRADE

FRISCO CONTACT MINE

21

IMPERIAL MINE

FRISCO

KING DAVID MINE

GARRISON

21

WASH

FRISCO (GHOST TOWN)

MILFORD

SQUAW SPRING

SCALE   KMS
0   4   8

9. Indian Peak, Needle Range

Location Not much is known of or written about mountains in the Great Basin of Utah. It's a dry are with few rivers or streams, thus almost void of population. There are only a few scattered ranches ar some mining activity and that's about it. But there are interesting mountains, some of which are attractive to climbers. One of these areas is the Needle Range. It's in the southwest part of the state west of Milford about 80 kms. Highest summit is Indian Peak, 2984 meters.

Geology Indian Peak has the appearance of a volcanic cone, but is not. However, it is made up of Tertiary volcanic rocks of various kinds — rhyolite, tuff and basalt. Just to the south and to the northwes of the peak are two small intrusive bodies which explain the existence of former mining activity.

Access The best way of getting to Indian Peak is to drive west out of Milford on State Highway 21 pas the old Frisco mining town ruins to between mile posts 41 and 42. There a good graveled road run south for 18 kms to where a BLM sign points out the road running southwest to the Indian Peak Stat Game Management Area. The graveled road running between Highway 21 and Lund is well-maintaine allowing cars to pass at highway speeds. Go prepared with plenty of gasoline.

Trail Information There are no trails in the area, only 4WD tracks and the few improved roads leading to the Game Management Area. This state game area was bought by the Utah Fish and Game Dept. in 1957 from the Piute Indians. Since then the Fish and Game Dept. has introduced and maintained an ell herd surrounding the peak. The only live or running water here is Indian Creek, which flows for about (kms. To get to the peak follow the arrows on the map. At the junction near the house, one can make a loop on the road running east of the peak. The best route, with the least amount of bushwhacking, is up a small canyon southeast of the summit. Walk up a 4WD road, then use game trails which pass ar excellent spring, eventually curving to the north. Follow the fence north to the summit. There must be bristlecone pines here, but the author failed to see any on this route. A northeast ridge route looks good also.

Best Time and Time Needed One could climb Indian Peak as early as the beginning of May and perhaps as late as early November. If a vehicle is taken to the very base of the peak, then it's a half day to the summit, a full day if the car is left near the house.

Campgrounds There are no campgrounds here, but many good campsites along Indian Creek. Many cattle graze the area, so the best drinking water is higher up in the creek.

Maps Utah Travel Council Map 5 — Southwestern Utah, U.S.G.S. maps Wah Wah Mts. South (1:100,000), Buckhorn Spring, Pinto Spring (1:24,000)

Indian Peak as seen from the Pine Valley Road. It's 8 kms to the peak (35mm lens).

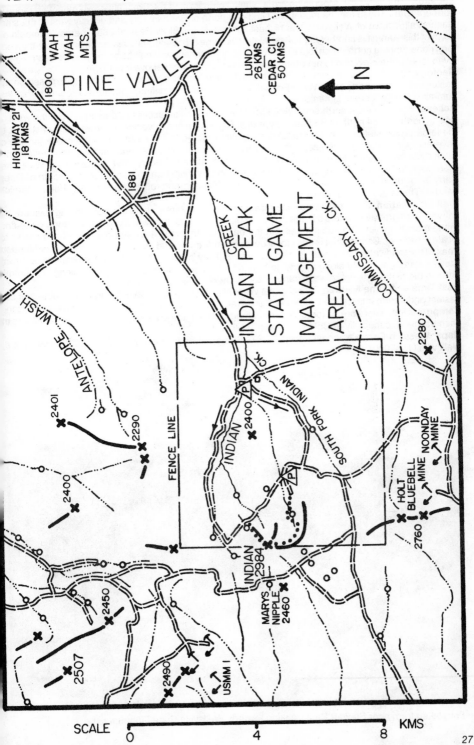

SCALE

0   4   8   KMS

10. Box Elder Peak, Wellsville Mountains

Location The Wellsville Mountains are a small, compact and relatively unknown mountain range ii northern Utah. These are the mountains lying due north of Brigham City and directly west of the sma Cache Valley town of Wellsville. The highest summit is Box Elder Peak at 2857 meters. Immediatel north of this summit is another high peak, Wellsville Cone, 2852 meters. This range is no more than on long ridge running north-south, but it receives heavy winter snows and has an impressive eastern face Even though the elevation is not great, the highest summits are above timberline.

Geology The Wellsville Mountains have been thrust upwards by a number of faults. Exposed on th eastern slopes are parts of the Wells Formation, which is almost entirely limestone. Around the highes summit is the Lodgepole Limestone.

Access Because it's a north-south ridge, there are three main access routes. First from the west. I driving north on I-84 north of Brigham City, exit at Honeyville and drive through town to the east side, t the large power station. From there take the gravel road north for about 2 kms, then look for one o several rough roads heading east to the mouth of the canyon. The road ends at a livestock water tank But a route on the east slopes has the best trails and is more scenic, so drive to the town of Wellsville then north to Mendon. From north Mendon one can drive west on a dirt road to the mouth of Deep Canyon, or drive in a southwesterly direction from Mendon and follow the signs to "Forest Service Lands". These are the three points of entry.

Trail Information From the Honeyville side and the water tanks, there's a trail running east up the canyon, but it gradually peters out and may be impossible to find. If, or when you lose it, simply route-find to the main ridge and the summit trail. On the east side the trails are more often used and easier to locate. The Deep Canyon trail is easy to follow as it winds its way up the canyon to a pass near Mendon Peak. The Coldwater Lake Trail is also well-used. They meet on the ridge at Stewart Pass. From Stewart Pass walk south along the trail to Youngs Cabin and spring, or simply walk along the summit ridge to the highest peaks. Always carry water as there's none on the ridge.

Best Time and Time Needed The climb of Wellsville Peak is an all day affair from any route, but the easiest and shortest is via the Coldwater Lake Trail. Mid-June through October is the hiking season.

Campgrounds There are no forest service campgrounds in the area, but there are good campsites at each trailhead, especially at Coldwater Lake Trailhead.

Maps Wasatch-Cache National Forest, U.S.G.S. maps Logan, Tremonton (1:100,000), Honeyville, Wellsville (1:24,000)

Foto taken from near Stewart Pass, looking towards Wellsville Cone (35mm lens).

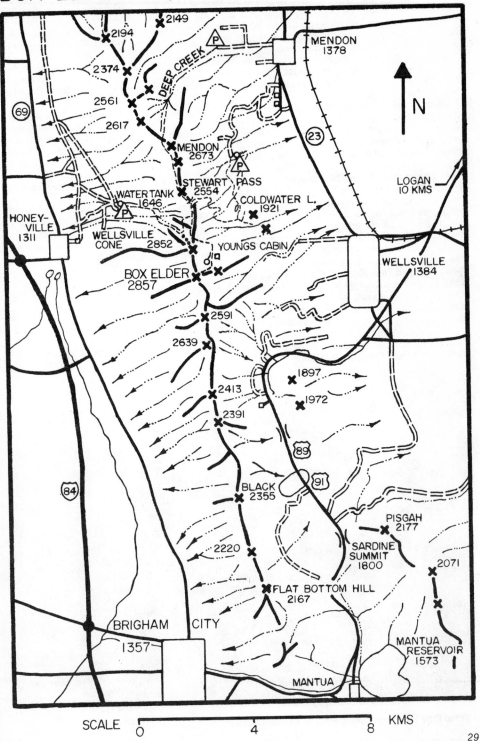

SCALE

0   4   8   KMS

11. Naomi Peak, Bear River Mountains

Location One of the most northerly ranges in the state of Utah is the Bear River Mountains. These mountains are located between Logan and Bear Lake. Parts of the range extend north into Idaho, but the higher and more interesting parts are on the Utah side of the line. The highest peak on the map is Naomi at 3042 meters. This is an easy peak to scale, but others such as Magog and Gog have steep sides and offer challenges to rock climbers.

Geology In the area of the highest summits the rock is limestone and in the basin above White Pine Lake, a type of Karst topography exists, complete with sink holes and caves. This is Utahs answer to Floridas Karst country. The limestone in question is part of the Lodgepole Limestone, Hyrum Dolomite, and Leatham Formations.

Access There are several roads into this area, but the most used and popular route is to drive up Logan Canyon east of Logan, heading in the direction of Bear Lake. At Tony Grove Campground, turn left or west, and drive up the paved road to Tony Grove Lake. This lake is in the area of high peaks and at an altitude of 2552 meters. Camping is not allowed at the lake, but there is a parking lot, and it's here most people park when they hike into White Pine Lake — one of the most scenic mountain places in Utah. It's also very crowded.

Trail Information From Tony Grove Lake one can walk northwest on a good trail to very near the summit of Naomi Peak. From the pass, simply walk south along the ridge. Also from Tony Grove Lake another much-used trail heads over the pass to the north and leads to White Pine Lake. From this lake, Magog and Gog can be climbed. The easiest route up Magog is a walk-up from the south. One could also reach this central part by walking up the trail from the end of either of the roads in Smithfield and High Creek Canyons. One could also walk up Cherry and White Pine Creeks as well as others, but other trails may not be as easy to locate. Most trails shown on the map are fairly well-used. All canyon bottoms have good water supplies.

Best Time and Time Needed For most it's a two hour hike to the top of Naomi Peak from Tony Grove Lake and perhaps less for Magog (from the south). Climbing Doubletop from the end of the road in High Creek Canyon is about a half-day hike.

Campgrounds There are plenty of campgrounds in Logan Canyon, including Tony Grove C.G., but these are generally crowded on weekends. One cannot camp at Tony Grove Lake, but backcountry camping is permitted everywhere.

Maps Wasatch-Cache National Forest, U.S.G.S. maps Logan (1:100,000), Richmond, Naomi Peak, Smithfield, Mount Elmer (1:24,000)

White Pine Lake with Magog Peak in the background (35mm lens).

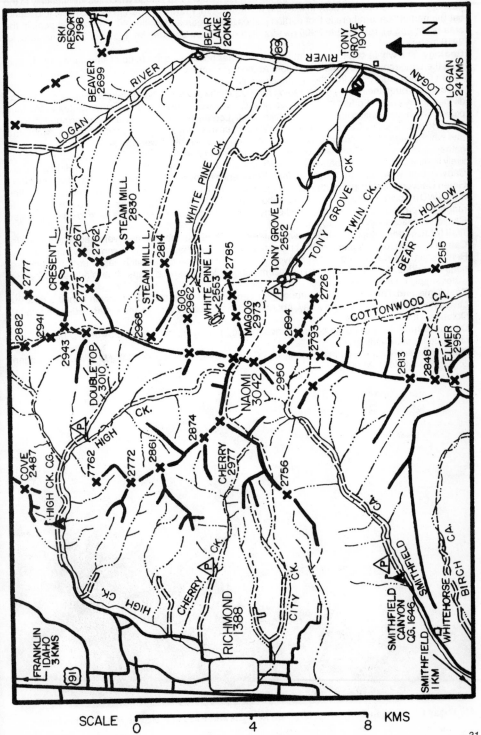

SCALE   0   4   8   KMS

12. Mt. Logan, Bear River Mountains

Location This is the second of two maps covering the Bear River Range which lies immediately to the east of Logan and Cache Valley in extreme northern Utah. Parts of the range extend north into Idaho, but the part of concern here is that portion just east of Logan and Smithfield. The highest peak in the area is Mt. Logan, reaching to 2960 meters. In the northern sections Mt. Elmer is 2950 and Jardine, 2916 meters.

Geology The whole of Mt. Logan, at least the higher portions, is made up of limestone rock, largely from the Lodgepole Limestone Formation. At the very summit, the Round Valley Limestone appears. Logan Canyon cuts deep into the Hyrum Dolomite.

Access Through the middle of this region runs US Highway 89 up Logan Canyon. This good highway divides the area, and offers good access points. However, there are many other routes to the high peaks. For those wanting to have a good hike up Mt. Logan, the best way is via the Logan subdivision of River Heights, and Dry Canyon. There's a 4WD road up this canyon, but that gradually fades away into a trail which leads to the summit. On top of Mt. Logan is a radio tower and some kind of station for gathering information. There is also a 4WD road to the top from the Millville Canyon side, but this is not likely to be of interest to climbers or hikers. Mt. Logan could also be climbed from Spring Hollow or Card Canyon, both within Logan Canyon, or from Providence Canyon. Mt. Jardine can best be climbed from Green Canyon, located just northeast of Logan. Within the canyon is a road, of which the upper section is for 4WD machines. Mt. Elmer can be climbed from either Birch or Dry Canyons on the west side of the range, or from the east and Cottonwood Canyon and campground. One would have to drive up Logan Canyon to reach this eastern route.

Trail Information Most trails in these mountains are good, but they are not over-used. The trail in Dry Canyon leading to the summit of Mt. Logan fades a bit near the top, but one can always find it easily. Remember, toward the top of the canyon, the trail makes several switch-backs up the prominent northwest ridge. All trails are shown on recent national forest service maps. One is advised to carry a water supply on most hikes.

Best Time and Time Needed A strong hiker can do Mt. Logan from Dry Canyon in half a day, but others will take the better part of a day. About the same is true for Jardine and Elmer. Mid-June through October is the hiking season.

Campgrounds Lots of public campgrounds in Logan Canyon, but they're crowded. Other canyons offer quieter surroundings.

Maps Wasatch-Cache National Forest, U.S.G.S. maps Logan (1:100,000), Mt. Elmer, Mt. Logan, Logan, Smithfield (1:24,000)

Mt. Logan right, Logan Canyon center; seen from Stewart Pass in Wellsville Mts. (105mm lens).

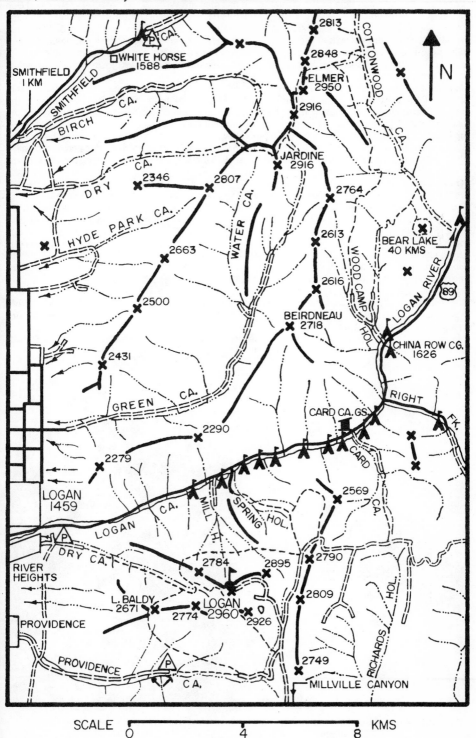

SCALE   0   4   8   KMS

13. Ben Lomond, Wasatch Mountains

Location The two mountain peaks of interest on this map are Willard Peak, at 2977 meters and Ben Lomond, a few meters lower, at 2961. These peaks lie directly north of Ogden in the northern Wasatch Mountains. There's a road to near the top of Willard Peak, so emphasis is placed more on Ben Lomond. What Timp is to Utah Valley and Provo, Ben Lomond is to Ogden and surrounding communities.

Geology The very steep and rugged western faces of Willard and Ben Lomond Peaks are the result of a part of the Wasatch Fault. The highest portions of these peaks are made up mostly of quartzite rock of both Cambrian and Precambrian ages.

Access For those interested in Willard Peak, and not much of a hike, then the easiest access route is to drive to Brigham City and Mantua, then go up Box Elder Creek to the south. This road leads to the Willard Basin just north of the peak. From the campground and small lake, a trail leads to the summit and to Ben Lomond. For those interested in a good hike, the normal route to the top of Ben Lomond is to drive up Ogden or North Ogden Canyon to the Ogden Valley and turn north. Continue north past Liberty to the Weber County North Fork Park and Campground. From the area of the horse corrals begins the trail to the top. One could also begin at North Ogden Pass, 1885 meters, and walk north along the Skyline Trail to Ben Lomond or Willard Peak.

Trail Information For the most part, the one major trail on this map is the Skyline Trail. This trail runs from the Willard Basin Campground south over Ben Lomond and Chilly Peaks and to North Ogden Pass, then south to Ogden Canyon, due east of Ogden. This is a very good trail and well-used. At the time of this writing, motorcycles were allowed on this trail. The other main trail is the one connecting North Fork Campground with the Skyline Trail and Ben Lomond. From the campground the trail zig zags up the slope, passing the ruins of Bailey Cabin where a small spring is located. There's also a short trail to the Cutler Spring located at the head of Cutler Creek. Carry water along the Skyline Trail.

Best Time and Time Needed The hike from North Fork Park to Ben Lomond is most of one day for most people. From North Ogden Pass to Willard Basin is generally an entire day's hike. Hiking season is from about mid-June through October.

Campgrounds Campgrounds in the area include two near Mantua, at North Ogden Pass, North Fork Park, and perhaps the best at Willard Basin. Lots of backcountry campsites, but you'll have to carry water, or camp at one of the springs.

Maps Utah Travel Council Map 4 — Northeastern Utah, and Wasatch-Cache National Forest, U.S.G.S. maps Ogden (1:100,000), Mantua, North Ogden, Huntsville (1:24,000)

From the summit of Ben Lomond, one has a fine view of Willard Peak to the north (35mm lens).

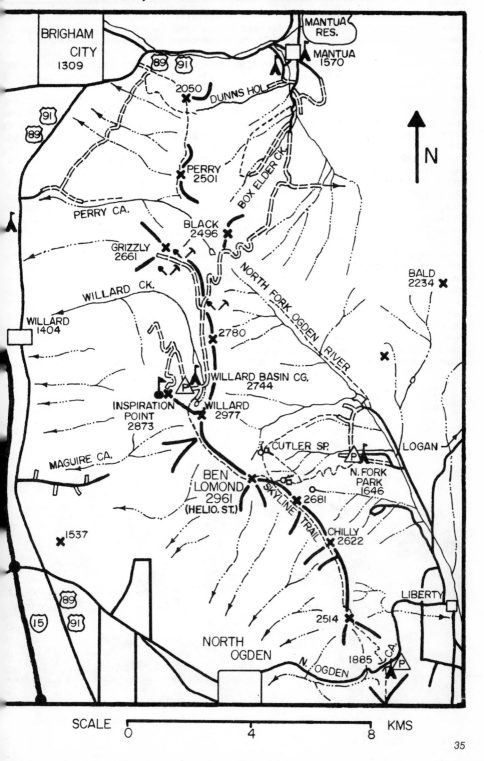

BRIGHAM
CITY
1309

MANTUA
RES.

MANTUA
1570

89 91

2050
DUNNS HOL

N

91
89

PERRY
2501

BOX ELDER CK.

PERRY CA.

BLACK
2496

GRIZZLY
2661

BALD
2234

NORTH FORK OGDEN RIVER

WILLARD CK.

WILLARD
1404

2780

WILLARD BASIN CG.
2744

INSPIRATION
POINT
2873

WILLARD
2977

CUTLER SP.

LOGAN

MAGUIRE CA.

N. FORK
PARK
1646

BEN
LOMOND
2961
(HELIO. ST.)

SKYLINE TRAIL

2681

CHILLY
2622

1537

LIBERTY

89

15 91

2514

NORTH
OGDEN

N. OGDEN

1885

LIBERTY CA.

SCALE   0   4   8   KMS

14. Mt. Ogden, Wasatch Mountains

Location Mt. Ogden is located directly east of Ogden and South Ogden, and between Weber and Ogden Canyons. This map covers another small area just to the north of Ogden Canyon, and up to the North Ogden Canyon. This section includes Lewis Peak and portions of the Skyline Trail. Mt. Ogden is the highest peak in the area at 2918 meters. The northeast slopes of this massif hold the Snow Basin Ski Resort.

Geology Fault lines run everywhere in this mapped area, especially in the northern parts. Most of the rock making up Mt. Ogden is Precambrian in age and composed of quartzite and other metasediment rocks.

Access There are several access points into this area from the cities of Ogden and North Ogden. One can also drive east up Ogden Canyon to the Pineview Reservoir, then turn southwest and end the drive at Snow Basin; or drive east out of North Ogden and over North Ogden Pass into the Ogden Valley, in which Pineview Reservoir is the central attraction. One can also enter some parts of the massif from Mt. Green.

Trail Information For those interested in a good hike and exercise, the logical route to the top of Mt. Ogden is via Taylor Canyon, Malans Peak and the west face of the peak. This trail begins at the eastern end of 27th Street. It enters Taylor Canyon, and zigzags up the slope to the top of Malans Peak. Then it goes down to the stream in the upper part of Waterfall Canyon. The trail gradually dies out, but continue up the gully and to the top via the west face of Mt. Ogden. One can also reach the top via the ski runs of Snow Basin. An interesting ridge hike is the Skyline Trail extending from Ogden to North Ogden Canyons. Carry water on this route, as much of the trail is on a ridge. This is a very popular trail and is in good condition.

Best Time and Time Needed For the average hiker, the Malans Peak Trail up Mt. Ogden takes the better part of one day. If one were to drive to Snow Basin and hike from there to any of the higher peaks, it is a very easy half-day hike. If hiking from Ogden to North Ogden Canyon on the Skyline Trail, that is one full day for most. The hiking season is from early June through October, depending on the route taken.

Campgrounds The only designated forest service campsites in the area of this map are located at the top of North Ogden Canyon, and in Snow Basin called Maples Campground. If one is using the Malans Peak Trail, there are many good campsites in the Upper Malans Basin at the head waters of Waterfall Creek. There's plenty of water in Waterfall Canyon, except higher up where the trail fades.

Maps Wasatch-Cache National Forest, U.S.G.S. maps Ogden (1:100,000), Ogden, Snow Basin, North Ogden, Huntsville (1:24,000)

From summit of Mt. Ogden. Snow Basin lower left. Not high, but above timberline (17mm lens).

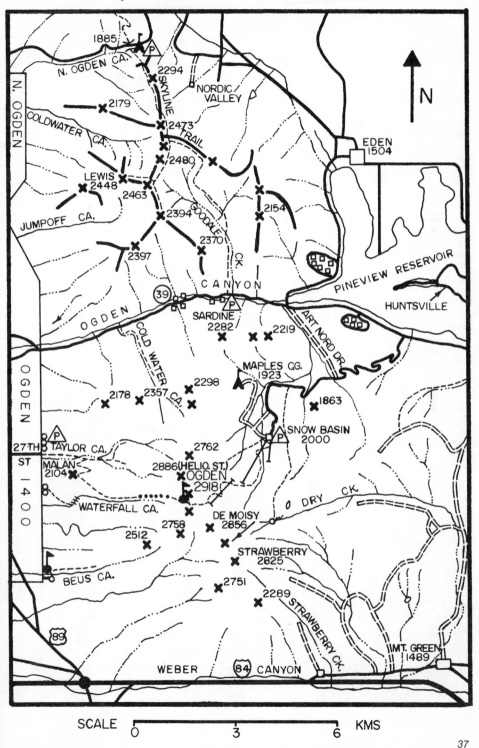

15. North Francis Peak, Wasatch Mountains

Location The region covered by this map is that part of the Wasatch Mountains between Farmington and Weber River Canyon. At this point the range consists of a single north-south ridge. The highest point on this ridge is what the author calls North Francis Peak, 2959 meters. This is not to be confused with Francis Peak, at 2911 meters, which lies further to the south on the same ridge and which has a road to the summit.

Geology The rock seen in these peaks is a mixture of quartzite and other metamorphic rock Precambrian in age. It's the Big Cottonwood and Farmington Canyon Formations here.

Access While one can drive to the summit of Francis Peak, it's also possible to hike up to this ridge from the west and Highway 89. If using the Francis Peak Road and the Skyline Drive, one must begin at the north end of Farmington, or possibly east of Bountiful on 1300 East Street. If climbing North Francis from the valley floor is anticipated, then one should get off the freeway at Lagoon, travel north on US Highway 89 and use one of the trails in the canyons between Fruit Heights and the Hill Field Road. One problem you may encounter in hiking here is the growing number of new roads and homes east of the highway. Any detailed information given here will surely change quickly.

Trail Information Probably the easiest way to reach North Francis, besides using the Francis Peak Road, is to find the north end of Valley View Drive and look for public approach roads leading to a trail on the ridge just south of Hobbs Canyon. At about 3200 North on Highway 89 is a posted private road — which makes the easiest point of access. One may have to ask at a home for a route to the trail which is on national forest lands beyond the homes. This trail zig zags up the ridge, then turns south and ends at a sheep herders cabin in the cirque basin. From the cabin, one must route-find up the slopes and along the ridge to North Francis. There's water at about 2425 and 2725 meters on this trail. Adams Canyon can also be used to climb to the ridge and summit trail. This trail begins just south of where Gentile Street intersects Highway 89. One may have to make inquiries locally as to the beginning or access to this trail. Another trail is the one leading up Baer Creek. This is just east of Fruit Heights and Kaysville.

Best Time and Time Needed For the average person, a hike to the top of one or several of these ridge peaks is an all day affair. Strong hikers who know the access routes can do it in half a day. Carry water on all trails as the lower portions are usually warm while the ridge tops are always dry.

Campgrounds Bountiful Peak and Sunset Campgrounds are open, but crowded.

Maps Wasatch-Cache National Forest, U.S.G.S. maps Ogden (1:100,000), Kaysville, Peterson (1:24,000)

Sheepherders cabin on North Francis Peak makes fine shelter in bad weather (35mm lens).

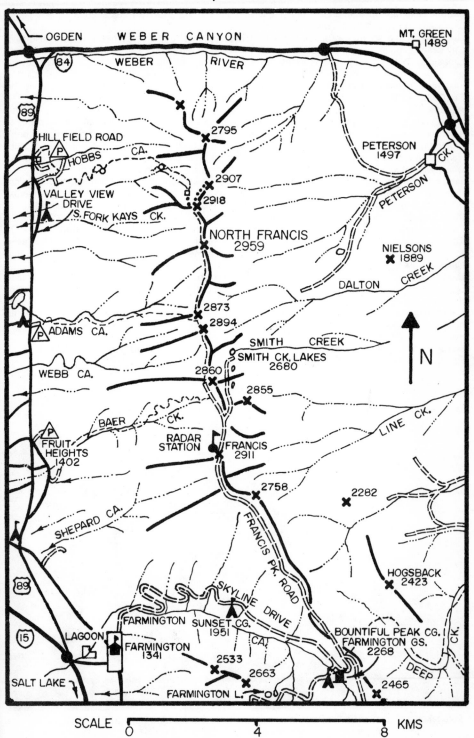

SCALE

0   4   8   KMS

16. Grandview Peak, Wasatch Mountains

Location This map includes some of the lesser known hiking areas in the Wasatch Mountains east of the Salt Lake Metropolitan area. The highest summit here is Grandview Peak at 2869 meters. These peaks are due east of Bountiful and North Salt Lake.

Geology Most of the rock formations here have been upturned and are now nearly vertical, at least in City Creek Canyon. Beginning in City Creek Canyon one sees these different formations: Maxfield Limestone, Tintic Quartzite, Ophir Formation and the Deseret Limestone. Right on top of Grandview and other summits of the Sessions Mountains one can observe parts of the Wasatch Formation, a mixture of limestone and quartzite and other rocks. Beneath the northern parts of this map lie the Pre-Cambrian Big Cottonwood Formation.

Access The easiest access road to Grandview Peak is up City Creek Canyon, but keep in mind this canyon is closed to camping, dogs and horses, and is closed at night. One must have reservations to enter the canyon. Call the Salt Lake City Dept. of Public Utilities for the latest restrictions and entry requirements. Because of the problems in City Creek, other routes are suggested, one being Mueller Park southeast of Bountiful. To reach these picnic sites drive east up 1800 South Street in Bountiful which ends at Mueller Park. Another less congested entry point would be North Canyon.

Trail Information If using City Creek Canyon, walk northeast along the creek until Cottonwood Gulch, then walk due north to the summit on an unmaintained trail. Perhaps some bushwhacking is needed here. If beginning at Mueller Park, cross the creek at the beginning of the park or use the second trail at the locked gate higher up. These trails meet higher up and take hikers to the ridge top above City Creek. From there one can walk down North Canyon, or continue northeast along the ridge to Grandview Peak. There's supposed to be a trail from Mueller Park to the Sessions Mountains Ridge, but the author failed to locate that trailhead. All of the trails on this map are well-used and usually maintained by the Wasatch National Forest.

Best Time and Time Needed One can hike in the canyon bottoms from April through November, but to climb the higher peaks without a lot of snow, hike from about June 1 through October. All hikes here are day hikes.

Campgrounds There is no camping allowed in City Creek Canyon or in any of the canyon bottoms near the metropolitan area. Backcounty camping is allowed only in areas in the eastern portions on this map. Plan on day hikes only.

Maps Wasatch-Cache National Forest, U.S.G.S. maps Salt Lake City (1:100,000), Mountain Dell, Porterville, Bountiful Peak, Fort Douglas (1:24,000)

Foto taken just above Mueller Park, of Sessions Mts. left, Grandview right (35mm lens).

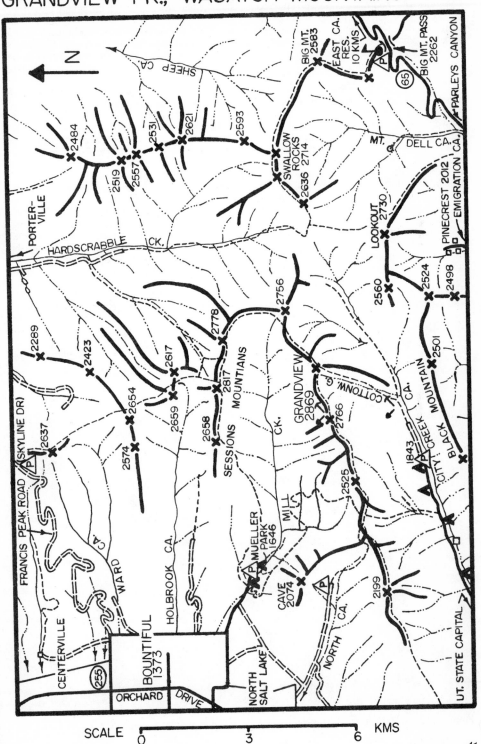

SCALE

0　　　　　3　　　　　6　　KMS

17. Mt. Olympus, Wasatch Mountains

Location The mountains shown on this map are those almost directly east of the central part of Salt Lake Valley. In particular, most of the peaks here are those which lie between Mill Creek and Big Cottonwood Canyons. The peaks here are not as high as those to the south near the ski resorts, but the area has some good, well-used paths which make for good hiking right on Salt Lake City's back doorstep. The highest peak in the group is Gobblers Knob, at 3124 meters, followed closely by Mt. Raymond at 3122 meters. However, the most famous mountain in this area is Mt. Olympus, only 2752 meters.

Geology On the south slopes of Raymond and Gobblers Knob the Big Cottonwood Formation is exposed while the summits are often Tintic Quartzite. Lots of rugged cliffs on Mt. Olympus.

Access Access to this region is fast and easy. The main approach road is the one running up Mill Creek Canyon. Almost all peaks on this map can be reached from some point along this paved and busy highway. But for the two highest peaks, the fastest way to the top is probably from one of the trails in Big Cottonwood Canyon. One can also reach Mt. Aire from Interstate Highway 80 in Parley's Canyon, then south up Mt. Aire Canyon. Some hikes can be started in Lambs Canyon, but very few. Mt. Olympus can be scaled by parking on Wasatch Boulevard at the mouth of Tolcats Canyon.

Trail Information As just mentioned, the way to the top of Mt. Olympus is via Tolcats Canyon. Park at the sign indicating the beginning of the trail on about 6300 South Wasatch Boulevard. It's a good trail and well-used. One may find water along the way, but that depends on the time of year. Carry water. To climb Mt. Raymond, the best starting point is beside Hidden Falls, not far up Big Cottonwood at the top of the "S" curve. This good trail cuts across the head of Elbow Fork, then along the south side of the peak. The last part of the route is likely easiest up the south face of the peak. One could continue along this same path and eventually end up at the pass west of Gobblers Knob. From there it's an easy hike to the summit from the west. Gobblers Knob can also be scaled from the trail going up Butlers Fork. Climb Grandeur Peak from Church Fork in Mill Creek Canyon, and Mt. Aire from Mt. Aire Canyon.

Best Time and Time Needed From the Salt Lake Valley most mountain climbs here are one full day. Carry water when walking on ridge routes. Hike here from early June through October, although one will find lots of snow on the higher peaks early in the season.

Campgrounds In recent years campgrounds have been changed to picnic sites, so there's really no camping in either of these canyons except in the backcountry.

Maps Wasatch-Cache National Forest, U.S.G.S. maps Salt Lake City (1:100,000), Sugarhouse, Mt. Aire (1:24,000)

From the trail to Mt. Raymond. The southwest face of Raymond (35mm lens).

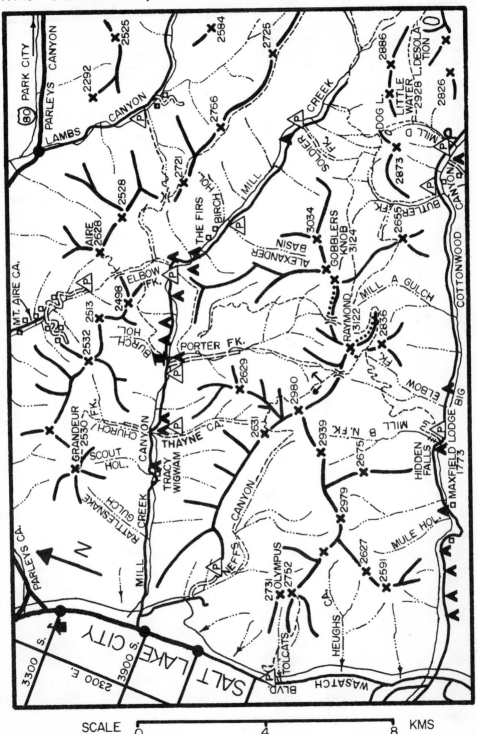

SCALE 0 — 4 — 8 KMS

18. Twin Peaks, Wasatch Mountains

Location The area covered by this map is that portion of the Wasatch lying due east of Sandy and Midvale in the Salt Lake Valley. It's also the high area between Big and Little Cottonwood Canyons, and is just west of Utah's major ski resorts. The highest summit on this map is Twin Peaks, with the highest peak to the east at 3454 meters. Probably the best known summit is Dromedary Peak at 3386 meters, just east of Twin Peaks. Other well-known summits are Superior, Millicent and Kessler.

Geology This is an old mining area with lots of mine shafts about. The rocks you'll be walking on are mostly quartzite, shale, slates, etc., mostly from the Big Cottonwood Formation. Some granite is exposed on the Little Cottonwood Canyon side.

Access There are two major highways providing access to this group of peaks. One is the highway up Big Cottonwood Canyon. This road ends at the Brighton Ski Resort (except for a dirt road going over Guardsman Pass to Park City). The other is the road up Little Cottonwood Canyon. This highway ends at Snowbird and Alta Ski Resorts. Both are good highways and kept open year-round.

Trail Information None of the peaks shown on this map have trails all the way to their summits. However, as time goes on and climbing becomes popular, trails are emerging. Two routes can be taken to the summit of Twin Peaks. One is to walk from the Mill B Picnic Grounds and up Broads Fork. The trail fades out about half-way up, but when that happens, route-find to the saddle east of the peaks, then walk west along the ridge. Twins can also be climbed from the south and one of several gullies on the south face. Dromedary Peak can be scaled from Mill B South Fork and Lake Blanche. Begin this climb at the Mill B Picnic Grounds and take the good trail southeast. From Lake Blanche, walk southwest to a saddle east of the peak, then up the ridge to the summit. If one were to either walk up the old 4WD road in Mill D South Fork, or the prominent trail leading up and to the northwest out of Alta, one could reach the pass and climb Superior to the west, or Flagstaff to the east, by walking along the ridge. There are many trails around the high area between Brighton and Alta, so one of these can be taken when climbing such peaks as Millicent and Sunset.

Best Time and Time Needed All hikes in this region are of the one day variety, with a few being half-day hikes. Hike from late June through October.

Campgrounds One can camp anywhere in the back country, or at the Brighton, Spruces, Tanner Flat or the Albion Basin Campgrounds. All are especially crowded on weekends.

Maps Uinta, Wasatch-Cache National Forest, U.S.G.S. maps Salt Lake City (1:00,000), Brighton, Dromedary, Mt. Aire (1:24,000).

Dromedary Peak center, Twin Peaks right; seen from trail to Mt. Raymond (35mm lens).

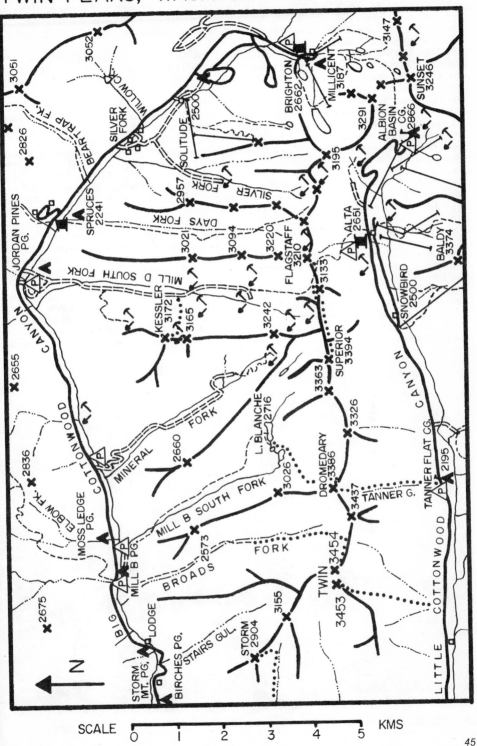

SCALE 0 1 2 3 4 5 KMS

19. Lone Peak, Wasatch Mountains

Location This map covers the mountains just to the southeast of Salt Lake City, directly east of Draper and north of Mt. Timpanogos. The highest peak is one of the American Fork Twins, at 3503 meters, but the best known summit is Lone Peak, at 3431 meters. Much of the area shown is part of the Lone Peak Wilderness Area.

Geology See the geologic cross section for better understanding of the geology of Lone Peak. The area covered by parts of Little Cottonwood Canyon, Lone and Matterhorn Peaks is granite, as a result of an igneous intrustion known as the Cottonwood Stock. Old mines mark its edge. Alta was once a mining town of about 5000 people.

Access Reach this area by one of four main access points. Little Cottonwood Canyon is on the north, Draper is to the west, then Alpine and American Fork Canyon and Tibble Fork Reservoir to the south. The northern routes are generally shorter with less elevation gain, but southern routes are less crowded. The Tibble Fork Reservoir and the Alta and Snowbird areas are heavily used.

Trail Information Climb Lone Peak from the trail going up Bells Canyon, or use the west or Draper Ridge route. Begin this just east of Draper on 12300 South, and one of two prominent ridges next to Corner Canyon. Another way is via Second East Street running northeast out of Alpine. From the end of the road, one must cross three streams before the trail or 4WD track is reached, which eventually ends at Lake Hardy. Climb Box Elder Peak from the prominent north-northeast ridge, which can be reached from Alpine and Dry Fork Creek, or from the Granite Flat Campground in American Fork Canyon. Climb the Little Matterhorn (Pfeiferhorn) from Alpine and Lake Hardy or from the Red Pine Lake basin. A longer route to this peak would be the trail in Bells Canyon. The simplest way to the American Fork Twins is to use the trail system out of the Snowbird Ski Resort. The second easiest way is via American Fork Canyon and either from Mineral Basin or from Silver Lake Flat Reservoir. Mill Canyon Peak can be scaled from one of two trails running east from the vicinity of Tibble Fork Reservoir, especially the trail up Mill Canyon.

Best Time and Time Needed Any of these hikes can be done in one day, especially those peaks near the ski resorts. Climbing Lone Peak from the Draper Ridge is perhaps the longest of any in this area, and one of the driest hikes as well. Generally speaking however, there are adequate supplies of water in all areas, especially in canyon bottoms. Climb from mid or late June through October.

Campgrounds One can camp at Tanners Flat or Albion Basin Campgrounds in Little Cottonwood Canyon, or at one of many crowded sites in American Fork Canyon.

Maps Uinta, Wasatch-Cache National Forest, U.S.G.S. maps Salt Lake City, Provo (1:100,000), Draper, Dromedary Peak, Brighton, Lehi, Timpanogos Cave (1:24,000)

From the Second Homongog on the south slopes of Lone Peak (35mm lens).

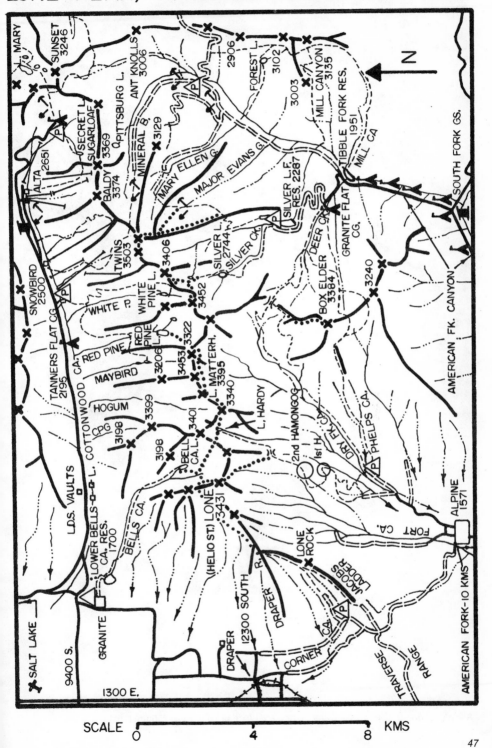

SCALE 0 — 4 — 8 KMS

A winter scene in upper Bells Canyon, and east face of Lone Peak (50mm lens).

Winter climbing is popular in Little Cottonwood Canyon, near White Pine Lake (50mm lens).

This campsite is located near Red Pine Lake in Little Cottonwood Canyon (50mm lens).

20. Mt. Timpanogos, Wasatch Mountains

Location Mt. Timpanogos, or *Timp* as it's called locally, is the dominating mountain at the north end of Utah County. It overlooks the entire valley and is the second highest peak in the Wasatch Mountains at 3582 meters.

Geology Timp is a huge hulk of a mountain built almost entirely of limestone. The bedding still remains horizontal, despite having been thrust upwards so high. The dominant formation seen here is the fossil filled Oquirrh Formation.

Access To reach the Aspen Grove Trail, the most popular route on the mountain, drive up Provo Canyon to Wildwood, turn left or north, and proceed up that canyon past Sundance Ski Resort until coming to the Aspen Grove Campground. The second most popular route up the mountain is via the Timpooneke Trail which is on the north end of the mountain. Get to this trailhead via either Provo Canyon or the road up American Fork Canyon.

Trail Information The Aspen Grove Trail is heavily used and well-maintained. It zig zags up the valley past waterfalls to the small lake at the bottom of the Timp Glacier. The trail then goes in a westerly direction to a pass, and along the face and north ridge to the summit. A variation of this route is to walk up the glacier south of the lake and Timp Shelter, to a pass or col, then follow the trail along the ridge to the summit. The Timpooneke Trail is just as scenic, but is about 13 kms long as compared to about 11 kms for the Aspen Grove Trail. These two trails meet high on the mountain. A recommended hike would be to walk up one trail and down the other — but this would take a car shuttle of some kind, or a bit of hitch hiking. Good water supplies on both trails. Another more rugged route to the top is via Pleasant Grove and that city's water tanks just east of town. It begins as a trail up Battle Creek, but crosses a couple of old dirt roads. Then, without trail, one must walk up one of the avalanche gullies right to the top. Another route is to drive to the east end of either 20th or 16th North in Orem, and walk up the trail in Dry Canyon. Higher up when the trail fades, one can then walk up one of the canyons to the summit ridge. Little or no water on the last two routes.

Best Time and Time Needed Mid-July through October is the climbing season when using the Aspen Grove or Timpooneke Trails, but the southwest face routes can be climbed in June. Whichever route is taken, plan on a full day's hike.

Campgrounds Provo Canyon has no campgrounds, only picnic sites which are always congested. American Fork Canyon has many campgrounds, but it too is a popular place. Aspen Grove and Timpooneke Campground are best, but are often full. Backcountry camping is permitted.

Maps Uinta, Wasatch-Cache National Forest, U.S.G.S. maps Provo (1:100,000), Orem (1:62,500), Orem, Timpanogos Cave, Aspen Grove, Bridal Veil Falls (1:24,000)

From the Timp Shelter looking south up the Timp Glacier. Best hike in Utah (50mm lens).

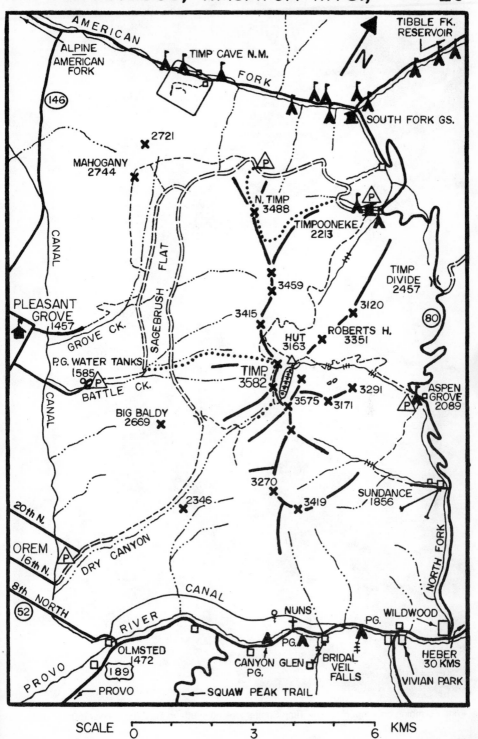

AMERICAN

ALPINE
AMERICAN
FORK

TIMP CAVE N.M.

FORK

TIBBLE FK.
RESERVOIR

N

(146)

SOUTH FORK GS.

× 2721

MAHOGANY
2744

P

N. TIMP
3488

TIMPOONEKE
2213

CANAL

SAGEBRUSH FLAT

× 3459

3415

TIMP
DIVIDE
2457

× 3120

(80)

PLEASANT
GROVE
1457

GROVE CK.

HUT
3163

ROBERTS H.
3351

P.G. WATER TANKS
1585

P

BATTLE CK.

TIMP
3582

3575
× 3171

× 3291

ASPEN
GROVE
2089

P

CANAL

BIG BALDY
2669 ×

× 2346

3270
×

3419

SUNDANCE
1856

20th N.

OREM
16th N.

P

DRY CANYON

NORTH FORK

8th NORTH

(52)

RIVER

CANAL

NUNS

WILDWOOD

PG.

OLMSTED
1472

PG.

CANYON GLEN
P.G.

BRIDAL
VEIL
FALLS

HEBER
30 KMS

PROVO

(189)

PROVO

SQUAW PEAK TRAIL

VIVIAN PARK

SCALE 0   3   6 KMS

Winter climbing on Timp. From the Timp Shelter looking south up the Timp Glacier (50mm lens).

Nearing the summit of Timp during a mid-winter climb. Summit to the left (50mm lens).

Winter climbing on Timp. Foto taken from east of the summit (50mm lens).

Summit of Timp, seen from the upper Timpooneke Trail and basin (50mm lens).

October Scene. North face of Timp's North Peak (50mm lens).

From the summit of Timp's North Peak, looking SE along summit ridge (50mm lens).

21. Cascade Peak, Wasatch Mountains

Location Cascade Peak lies directly east of Orem and northeast of Provo. This is the mountain with a large western face and high cliffs. It's also the birthplace of Bridal Veil (Creek) Falls, which can be seen from Provo Canyon. The mountain has several peaks over the 3000 meter level with the highest being 3326 meters.

Geology The entire mountain known as Cascade Peak is made up of the Oquirrh Formation. By far the most dominant rock seen here is limestone, but with small amounts of chert, shale and quartzite. The big west face is solid limestone.

Access The two main ways of reaching Cascade Peak are both from Provo Canyon. Drive up the canyon and about 1 km before reaching Springdell, turn right or south, and follow the Pole Canyon road (Squaw Peak Trail) past Hope Campground and to near a quarry at the bend of the road as shown. For the second access road, drive further up Provo Canyon and turn right or south at Vivian Park. This is the South Fork of Provo River. Stop at the picnic grounds near where Bunnels Fork meets South Fork. Use a trail to avoid the private property at the ranch. Higher up the land is public. Make inquiries at the mouth of Bunnells Fork for permission to cross this short stretch of private land. The mouth of Spring Hollow is completely blocked off to public access, but the upper canyon is forest service land.

Trail Information Probably the most scenic route to Cascade Peak is via Bunnells Fork. The trail in this canyon goes to the upper basin, then turns south and into Spring Hollow. Once in the upper basin simply route-find to the summit. The shortest walk to the top is via the quarry marked 2296 meters on the southwest corner of the mountain. From that spot, bushwhack up the slopes to the summit ridge, then walk north to the highest point. One can also ride the lift to the top of Bridal Veil Falls where a trail-of-sorts is being developed for hikers. For rock climbers, this may be one of the better climbs in the state, especially on the west and north faces. The big gully on the south face has some interesting routes as well.

Best Time and Time Needed Most climbers or hikers can do this peak in one long day by using the Bunnells Fork route, or about half a day for the Bridal Veil Falls or the southwest corner routes. Mid-June through October is the climbing season.

Campgrounds The only forest service campgrounds in the area are the Hope and Rock Canyon Campgrounds. However, one can camp in many places along the Squaw Peak Trail. Much of South Fork along the paved road is private land.

Maps Uinta National Forest, U.S.G.S. maps Provo (1:100,000), Bridal Veil Falls (1:24,000)

From the top of Lion Head Mt., one can see both Timp and south face of Cascade Peak (35mm lens).

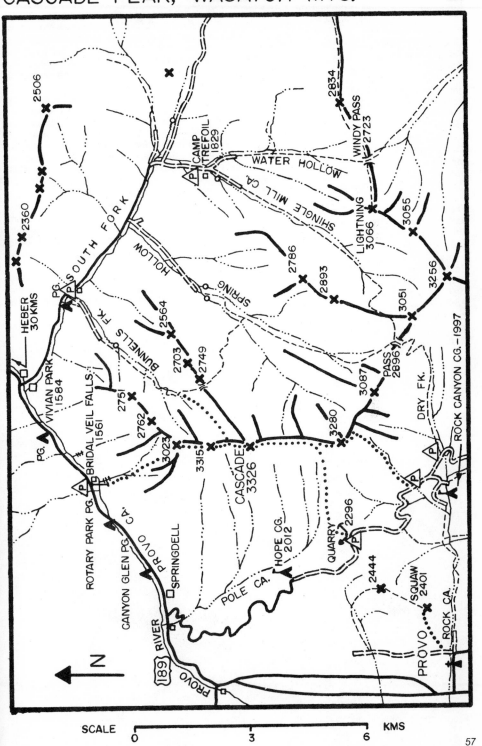

SCALE

0   3   6   KMS

22. Provo Peak, Wasatch Mountains

Location Provo Peak is the highest summit which rises to the east of Provo. There are four smaller mountains or foothills to Provo Peak and they are: Squaw Peak, "Y", Maple and Buckley Mountains. Provo Peak is the highest point along a ridge which stretches from Springville to Provo Canyon.

Geology Provo Peak is a limestone mountain with the Oquirrh Formation prominently exposed. The foothill peaks are also mostly limestone, but from different formations.

Access For Provo Peak and all of its subsidiary peaks, the best means of access is the road which connects the Left Fork of Hobble Creek and Provo Canyon. This is called the Squaw Peak Trail. It's a good road and open for about 4 months each year. For the four foothill peaks, it's usually best to walk up from one of many streets in downtown Provo, and up either Rock, Slide or Slate Canyons. The Left Fork of Hobble Creek would normally be a fine access point, but the land near the paved highway in that canyon is all private and one must have permission from land owners to pass to the forest service lands further up the mountain. Therefore, it's recommended that all climbing be done from the western slopes.

Trail Information There are good and well-used trails in the major canyons east of Provo. There are many hikers in the area, but none of the peaks actually have trails to their summits. Climb Squaw Peak from the mouth of Rock Canyon, and Y and Maple Mountains both from along the trail in Slide Canyon. Buckley Mountain can be climbed easiest from the Squaw Peak Trail Road, or from Slate Canyon and the north face. For Provo Peak, one can walk all the way from Provo, but that's a two day hike for most. The easiest way is to drive on the Squaw Peak Trail to where the west ridge intersects the road. From that point there's an old track up the mountain. After a ways, simply follow the west ridge to the summit. One could also walk up Burn Hollow, a northern route. A longer and more strenuous hike would be to walk from the mouth of Spring Canyon near Springville, along the prominent south ridge. This would be a very long and dry climb.

Best Time and Time Needed If one drives to the base of the west ridge of Provo Peak, it's only a couple of hours' walk to the top. To climb any of the "foothill mountains", it's an all day walk for the average hiker. Hiking season is from mid-June through October, but earlier and later, for hikes in the foothill mountains.

Campgrounds Only the Rock Canyon Campground is a designated campsite, but there are many places in which to camp. There are also many springs in the canyons.

Maps Uinta National Forest, U.S.G.S. maps Provo (1:100,000), Bridal Veil Falls, Springville (1:24,000)

From upper Bunnel's Fork on Cascade Peak, looking south to Provo Peak (50mm lens).

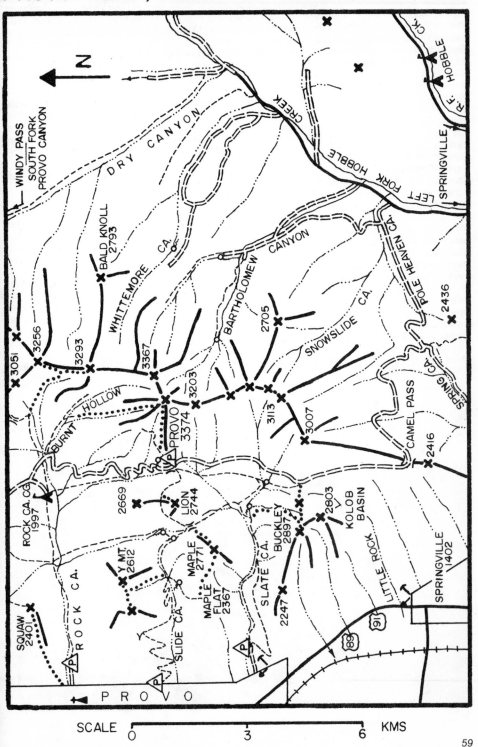

SCALE

0   3   6   KMS

23. Spanish Fork Peak, Wasatch Mountains

Location Spanish Fork Peak is one of the more prominent peaks seen in Utah Valley. It's located just east of Mapleton, which is just south of Springville and east of Spanish Fork. Its elevation is 3107 meters. Some people in Mapleton know the mountain as Monument Peak, and in the past there has been an annual hike to the summit.

Geology Spanish Fork Peak is almost entirely made up of the Oquirrh Formation. The rock is a combination of limestone and quartzite for the most part. Notice the flat bench lying along the west face. That's the highest shoreline deposits left from Lake Bonneville. These shoreline features are common to nearly all mountains in western Utah.

Access Access to the normal route to Spanish Fork Peak is via Mapleton. From Mapleton, drive east on 1200 North Street. This paved road heads up Maple Canyon to the Whiting Campground. Above the campground it's a rough road, but one which can be negotiated by any car, up to as far as the Dibbles Canyon area. If one is using the Pace Hollow route on the east side of the mountain, drive up Spanish Fork Canyon to the Diamond Fork Road. Then turn northeast to the Palmyra Campgrounds. From the campgrounds turn northwest 'till the road ends.

Trail Information The normal route is via Maple Canyon and the Right Fork of Maple Canyon. Most cars should be parked on the north side of Maple Creek, then walk south up a 4WD road which lasts only about 1 km. From there the well-used trail heads south up the canyon. Higher up is a large cirque basin where the Maple Canyon Lake lies. This is a good area for camping if an overnight trip is anticipated. The trail then zig zags up the slope to the west until the ridge is reached, then the trail more or less follows the ridge to the summit. Plenty of water available on the trail below the ridge. Perhaps the second best route, and one which always affords a good view of Utah Valley, is to climb the prominent west ridge immediately north of Crowd Canyon. There's only a short section with oak brush to walk through, which makes it an easy walk. There's no water on this route. Other possible routes are Wind Rock Ridge — Sterling Hollow, Pace Hollow, and Dibbles Canyon. These routes are mentioned, as the USGS maps show trails in these areas.

Best Time and Time Needed Any route on Spanish Fork Peak can be climbed in one day, but overnight hikes are enjoyable in Maple Canyon. The west ridge route could be climbed in May or November, but the Maple Canyon Trail is open from mid-June to October.

Campgrounds National forest campgrounds are Whiting in Maple Canyon (but it's always crowded) and Palmyra and Diamond Fork Campgrounds on Diamond Fork.

Maps Uinta National Forest, U.S.G.S. maps Provo (1:100,000), Spanish Fork Peak, Billies Mtn., Springville (1:24,000)

Foto taken from the south end of Provo Peak looking towards Spanish Fork Peak (35mm lens).

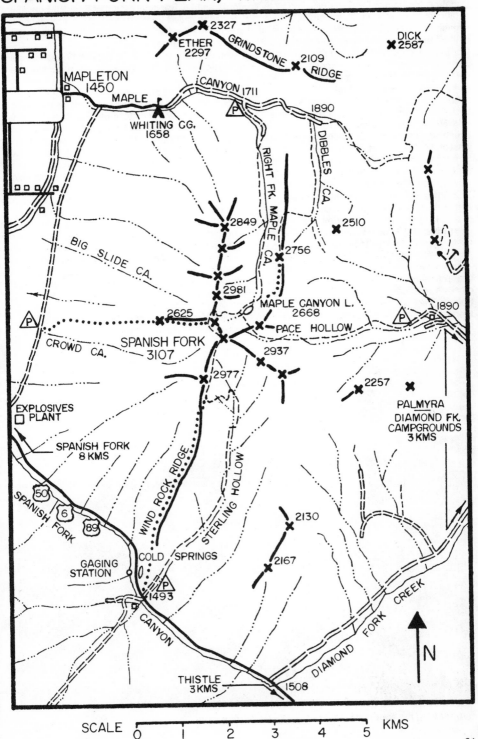

SCALE

0   1   2   3   4   5   KMS

24. Santaquin Peak, Wasatch Mountains

Location Santaquin Peak, usually known as Loafer Mountain, is located south of Spanish Fork and southeast of Payson in Utah County. This entire massif is called Loafer Mountain, and the highest summit is also known as Loafer. But the peak that is actually seen from Utah Valley is Santaquin Peak, at 3257 meters. Loafer Peak is just one meter higher at 3258 meters.

Geology Santaquin Peak and the whole of Loafer Mountain is made up of the Oquirrh Formation. It's mostly limestone, with some sandstone, chert and quartzite included. The Wasatch Fault runs along the northwest base of the mountain.

Access Because the northern and eastern parts of the mountain are privately owned lands, the only all national forest access route is from the area of Payson Lakes. Drive up Payson Canyon on the Nebo Loop Road to where the first road to the Payson Lakes turns right. On the opposite side of the highway is a 4WD road or trail. Follow this to the corral at the first pass, then go down a bit, then up Mud Hollow and eventually to the top of Santaquin Peak. One can also approach the mountain on a public access road west of Birdseye. A dirt road follows Bennie Creek. Walk west from the end of the road until Mud Hollow is reached, then proceed to the top. One can also use the Cutoff Trail as shown. Another possible route is up Bear Canyon, but that trail may be overgrown. With permission from land owners, one could also walk up from the end of the road in Loafer Canyon.

Trail Information Because much of the mountain is privately owned, the trails are little used and therefore sometimes difficult to locate. However, the Payson Lakes — Mud Hollow Trail is used enough to be self maintained. Trails are used mostly by cattle and cattlemen, and by deer and elk hunters.

Best Time and Time Needed A fast hiker can walk from Payson Lakes to the top in a couple of hours, but for most it turns out to be an all-day affair if driving time is included. Take water on the hike, as most trails are on ridge tops. If the Payson Lakes Trail is used, it's possible to climb the mountain in early June — that's because it's a southern ridge route. So the climbing season is June through October.

Campgrounds There are forest service campgrounds at Payson Lakes and Maple Bench and many other off road campsites along the Nebo Loop Road. One can also camp on the higher sections of Bennie Creek as that's national forest land.

Maps Utah Travel Council Map 7 — Northwestern Central Utah, Uinta National Forest, U.S.G.S. maps Nephi (1:100,000), Santaquin Peak (1:62,500), Spanish Fork, Spanish Fork Peak, Payson Lakes, Birdseye (1:24,000)

Foto showing the southeast slopes of Loafer Mt. (17mm lens).

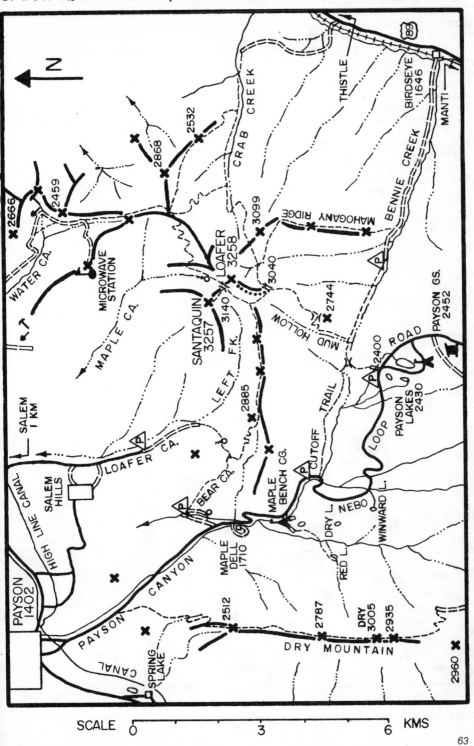

25. Mt. Nebo, Wasatch Mountains

Location Mt. Nebo is the most southerly of the Wasatch Mountain peaks and is located just to the east of Mona, and northeast of Nephi in Juab County. The mountain has three main summits running in a north-south direction. The highest is the North Peak, at 3637 meters. However, the two trails on the mountain stop at the southern peak, which is 3621 meters. On the south face of South Peak are the remains of the old Heliograph or Trigenometric Station dating back to the early 1880's.

Geology Mt. Nebo has many of the same characteristics as other high peaks in Utah County. Nearly the entire mountain is made up of the Oquirrh Formation which is mostly limestone. There are different formations exposed on Bald Mountain.

Access There are two main access routes (and trails) to the south summit. The most convenient is from the west and Mona, and up Willow Creek. From the end of Willow Creek Road a trail circles around the huge amphitheater and eventually reaches the south ridge. The other route is from the east and Salt Creek. Drive from Nephi east on Highway 132. Turn north at the KOA Campground and drive to the sign indicating the Nebo Trail and Andrews Creek. A 4WD road runs west for 1½ kms where the trail begins at the creek.

Trail Information Both trails mentioned are in good condition, but are not used as much as trails on Timpanogos for example. At the beginning of each trail, on Willow and Andrews Creeks, there is water available, but for the most part, nowhere else on the mountain. In early summer there are usually plenty of snow banks and some water at 2920 meters on the east face, as marked. For those preferring a trail-less hike, try the Cedar Ridge, or walk north on the Nebo Basin Trail, then climb direct to the summit on one of the high east face ridges. Nebo is the highest peak in the Wasatch Mountains. Its summit rises well above timberline.

Best Time and Time Needed The average hiker will need 4 to 6 hours for the climb to the summit on either trail — in other words, it's an all day hike. For those living in Utah Valley, it's an entire day's trip. For those living further from the mountain, camping at the mountain base might be best. Because the last part of the hike is on the south ridge, Mt. Nebo could be climbed from about the middle of June or July 1 through October in most years without the need for snow climbing equipment.

Campgrounds There are camping sites on Willow Creek which are less crowded than on Salt Creek. There are several national forest campgrounds on Salt Creek, and some very good undeveloped campsites on Andres Creek near the trailhead.

Maps Utah Travel Council Map 7 — Northwestern Central Utah, Uinta National Forest, U.S.G.S. maps Nephi (1:100,000), Santaquin, Santaquin Peak (1:62,500), Nebo, Nebo Basin (1:24,000)

The summit of Mt. Nebo. North Peak is in the distance (17mm lens).

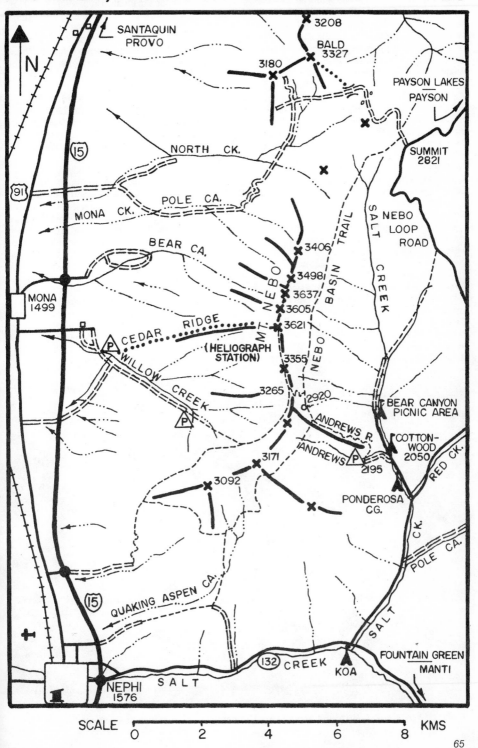

26. Fool Peak, Canyon Range

Location The Canyon Range is a little-known group of mountain peaks located in central Utah. They lie immediately to the east of the small town of Oak City, and a few more kms east of Delta. The highest summit is Fool Peak at 2962 meters.

Geology The greater part of the Canyon Range is composed of Precambrian metasediments, but as one approaches the summit region, the Tertiary formation, Fool Creek Conglomerate is found. These are for the most part rounded summits, but there are some very steep north and northeast faces to be found on the higher peaks.

Access Access is rather good to this range and it's relatively close to the southern part of the Utah metropolitan area. One can take I-15 south to Scipio, then use gravel and dirt roads to the steeper eastern face. Use the road up Little Oak Creek to gain access to the pass marked 2286 meters. However, the principal route of access is the paved road leading southeast and east out of Oak City. The pavement ends at the guard station and Oak Creek Campgrounds. From there it's a good gravel road up the canyon to the mouth of Lyman Canyon. The road ends just above that point. One can also use a much rougher road leading up Fool Creek. With a 4WD one can reach an altitude of 2500 meters west of Fool Peak.

Trail Information For those wanting to climb to the summit of Fool Peak, drive to the confluence of Lyman Canyon and park (or park in the area of Little Creek Campground). From Lyman Canyon, walk up to the pass on a good trail. From there, route-find up the ridge north to the summit. Or from Little Creek, walk up the 4WD road a ways, then turn east and bushwhack up a canyon. Near where there is a spring marked on the map, is a box canyon. From the end of it, regress 30 meters and climb the western slope to the top, then again use the canyon and cow trails to the summit. These two routes the author used. Later it was found that a real trail goes to the top from the end of North Walker Canyon and from the southern end of Fool Creek Canyon. This is apparently the route used by survey parties when they established an encampment near the summit. The only live running water is in the Oak Creek drainage.

Best Time and Time Needed If the easier west ridge trail is used, this is an easy half-day hike. If either of the other two routes are used, it could take most of one day for most people. Hike here from June 1 through October.

Campgrounds One reason for using the Oak Creek approach is the excellent campgrounds in that canyon. The best one is the Bowens Canyon C.G. situated in a large grove of ponderosa pine trees. But one can camp anywhere.

Maps Fishlake National Forest, Delta (1:100,000), Oak City, Scipio North (1:62,500)

Winter on Fool Peak, seen from Interstate 15. Note steep northeast face (105mm lens).

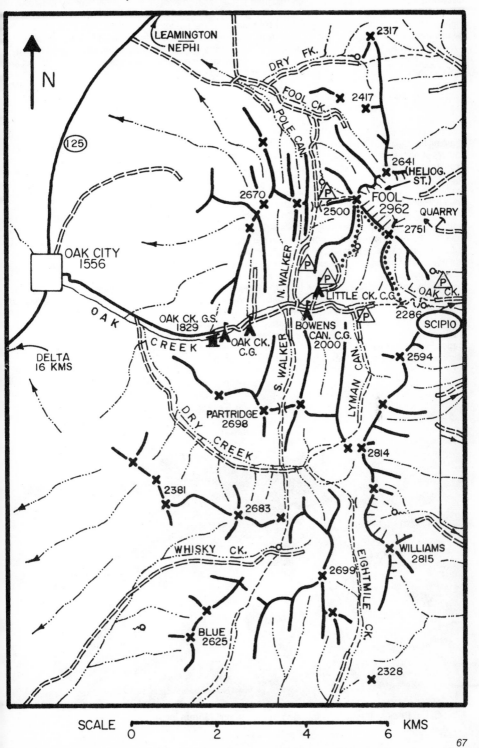

27. Mine Camp Peak, Pavant Range

Location The mountains included on this map are all located directly east of the central Utah town of Fillmore. The range is known as the Pavant Range and includes several summits over 3000 meters, the highest of which is Mine Camp Peak at 3116 meters. All the higher summits are located at or near the headwaters of Chalk Creek. The mountains in this range are rounded summits, and are used more by 4WDers than hikers, but there are a number of trails in the canyon bottoms which afford good hiking.

Geology Most of the rocks in this area are a mixture of quartzite and limestone. The Formations are Tintic Quartzite, North Horn Formation and the Maxfield Limestone.

Access Access is good, for both 4WD people and hikers with passenger cars. Those with 4WD vehicles can use a reasonably good road which runs northeast to southwest along one major ridge, most of which is at or near 3000 meters. This is used mainly by hunters. However, most traffic is up Chalk Creek to several recreation areas, mostly picnic sites. This road is paved for one quarter of the way to Pistol Rock Campground, then it's rough but passable to all cars. By using this road one can climb all the major summits on the map. There's also a reasonably good road up Meadow Creek to two campgrounds, from which begins a trail to the summit road.

Trail Information All trails, or at least those which begin in the Chalk Creek drainage, are well sign-posted and fairly well-maintained. These trails are used by cattlemen, boy scout groups and deer hunters, all of which are local people. As a result the place is not crowded. To climb Mine Camp Peak, drive to Pistol Rock Campground and park. Then follow the creek trail and signs to Paradise Canyon (it's the upper west fork of Bear Canyon). One can then use the Paradise Canyon route or turn left at that junction and eventually reach and follow a 4WD road up a ridge 'till an old service road is reached. From there walk cross country to the northwest to the top of Mine Camp. All these high ridges have old 4WD roads, but the canyons have trails only and are relatively primitive. To hike to the Catherine Peak area, use the Chalk Creek road, but look for one of two trailheads; one half-way up, the other near Copley's Cove Campground.

Best Time and Time Needed The hike up Mine Camp or Catherine can be done in one day by most hikers, but there are many excellent campsites, making overnight trips worthwhile. Hiking in this range can be done from the first part of June through October.

Campgrounds There are four listed campgrounds in Chalk Creek's South Fork, but are more like picnic sites than campgrounds. There are two campgrounds on Meadow Creek.

Maps Fishlake National Forest, U.S.G.S. maps Richfield (1:100,000), Fillmore, Richfield (1:62,500), Fillmore, Holden, Coffee Peak, Mt. Catherine (1:24,000)

Mine Camp Peak to the right, is forested to the summit (35mm lens).

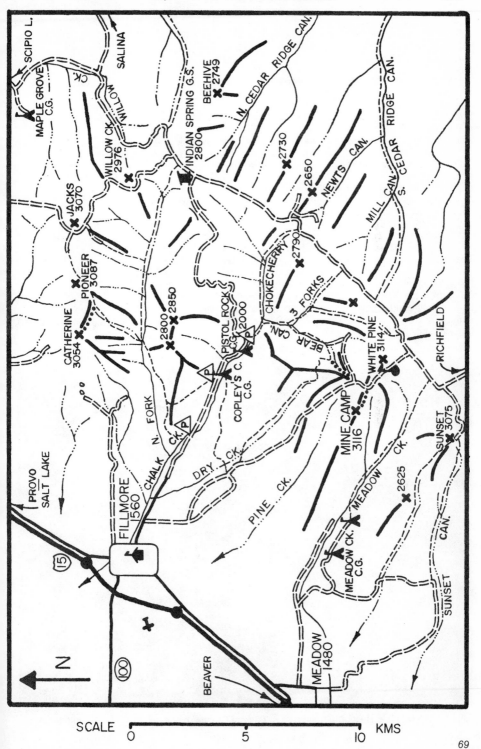

SCALE

0   5   10   KMS

28. Mt. Belknap, Tushar Mountains

Location The Tushar Mountains are a group of peaks among the highest in the state of Utah. They're in southwestern Utah just east of Interstate Highway 15 and Beaver. The highest summit is Mt. Delano at 3709 meters, but Mt. Belknap at 3699 meters is perhaps the most interesting peak to climb because of its steeper nature and the remains of an old Heliograph Station on its summit. These relics are among the best preserved of any seen by the author in the western USA. This map pretty well covers the entire range, from Signal Peak in the north to Circleville Mountain in the south.

Geology Almost all the rocks included on this map are volcanic in origin. Part of the area is Mt. Belknap Rhyolite, while in the southern part of the map around Birch Creek Peak, one finds the Muddy Creek Formation. There are many old mines in the northern part of the range especially around Copper Belt, Brigham and Bullion Peaks. Lots of old roads to scar the surface are in this area too. This is not a plateau, but true mountains.

Access The one major access route is the paved highway running between Beaver and the Mt. Holly Ski Resort and Puffer Lake. This road is used year-round. One can also get to this high country from Junction on the east side of the range on the same road, but the east side is steep, unpaved, and has hairpin turns even though it's well-maintained. There's also a road up from Marysvale, but it too is steep and bad at times making it a 4WD road.

Trail Information Few trails here, but there is one to the summit of Belknap on its southeastern side. Mt. Baldy can be reached from either Blue Lake or Mt. Belknap. There are many easy routes up the southwestern face of Delano just head that way from Big John Flat and route-find to the summit. There's an old 4WD track being made into a hiking trail from Big Flat Guard Station to City Creek Peak and Mt. Holly, and ending near Big John Flat. No trails to Circleville Mt., but it's easy to route-find everywhere.

Best Time and Time Needed The author climbed Delano, Belknap and Baldy in one long day, but most people may feel happy to do one or two in one day. This isn't really a back-packing area, just day hiking for the most part. Hike from mid-June through October.

Campgrounds There are several campgrounds along the Beaver River, but they require a fee. All other campgrounds shown are more primitive but free for usage. Good campsites everywhere.

Maps Fishlake National Forest, U.S.G.S. maps Beaver (1:100,000), Delano Peak (1:62,500), Circleville Mtn., Circleville (1:24,000)

Mt. Belknap with fine Heliograph ruins. As seen from Delano, highest in Tushars (105mm lens).

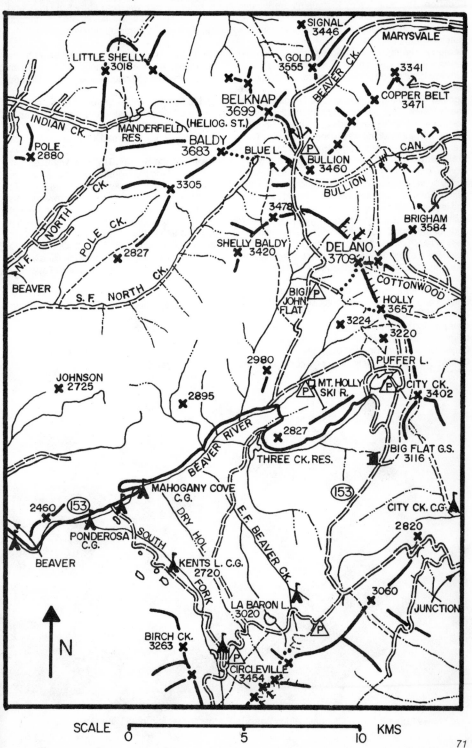

SCALE 0 5 10 KMS

29. Signal Peak, Pine Valley Mountains

Location The Pine Valley Mountains are located in the extreme southwestern corner of Utah, and directly north of St. George. The highest summit here is Signal Peak reaching a height of 3159 meters. There are many other summits very near this elevation, and the entire summit ridge is near the 3000 meter level.

Geology The map shows an escarpment on the east side, but this is not to be confused with the sandstone plateaus of most of Southern Utah. Most of the exposed rock at the higher elevations is an intrusive body called Quartze Monzonite. In a way it's similar to the laccolith mountains in the Colorado Plateau.

Access By exiting Interstate 15 at Leeds one can proceed to Oak Grove Campground at the head of Leeds Creek. This is the best road and access point on the east side. The other main access road is from the west. This road leads north out of St. George passing through Central and a place called Pine Valley. It's paved all the way to the Pine Valley Campground, at the end of the road. One can also reach the northern areas by using I-15 and exiting at New Harmony.

Trail Information There are two main trails here. One known as the Summit Trail is a well-used trail running from north to southwest making a half-moon arch. It runs along the highest portion of the range and is on the summit ridge almost all the way. This is the main trail that most hikers will encounter while hiking. There's also a trail system running along the eastern base of the high escarpment; however, this one is at a low elevation and is extra warm during the summer season. If you're out to reach the highest point, Signal Peak, then begin hiking at the Oak Grove Campground. A good, well-used trail leads up a ridge to the top and connects with the Summit Trail. There's no trail to the top of Signal Peak, but it's easy to reach after you pass a spring called Further Water (near the last "R" on Burger). One can also reach the summit ridge by using the Forsyth Creek Trail or a trail beginning just west of the Pine Valley Campground. Another trail leads out of the same campground and heads for the Whipple Valley to the northeast.

Best Time and Time Needed From either campground, Oak Grove or Pine Valley, this climb can be done in one day, but two day trips are common. Be aware of a lack of water on the Summit Trail. Hiking season here is June 1 through October.

Campgrounds Both campgrounds mentioned are improved and open most of the year. Oak Grove Campground is free for usage and likely the least crowded of the two.

Maps Utah Travel Council Map 5 — Southwestern Utah, Dixie National Forest, U.S.G.S. maps St. George (1:100,000), New Harmony (1:62,500), Saddle Mtn., Central East (1:24,000)

Foto shows Summit Trail on Summit Ridge passing Further Water (spring) (17mm lens).

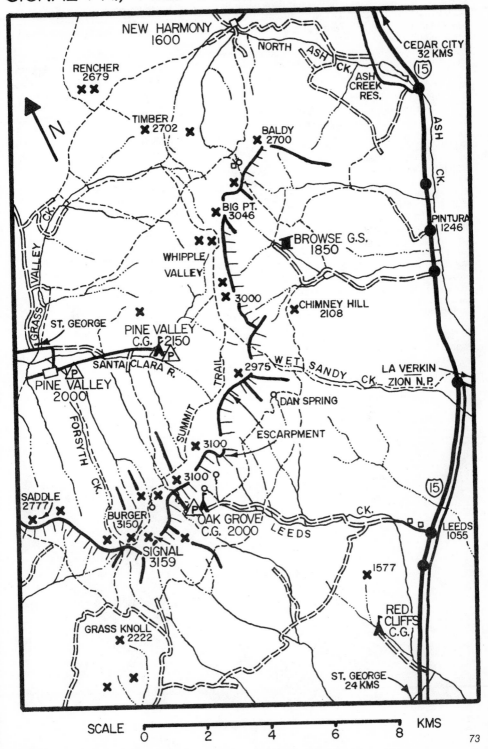

30. Bluebell Knoll, Boulder Mountains

Location The area covered by this map is known as the Boulder Mountains, the highest part of which is the Boulder Top. The Boulder Top is just west of the central part of the Capital Reef National Park and south of Loa, Bicknell and Torrey in south-central Utah. The highest point on the Boulder is Bluebell Knoll at 3453 meters.

Geology The Boulder Top has been eroded away on all sides leaving an escarpment as shown on the map. The top or rim of the plateau is about 3250 meters and has a drop of from 150 to 200 meters. The Top is made up of volcanic rock of Tertiary age.

Access The north slope of the Boulder Top can really only be reached from the north and the Fremont River Valley. Use Highway 24 which runs from Richfield to Loa, Hanksville, and on to Green River. From Teasdale or Torrey drive south on the paved road running to Boulder and Escalante, but turn right about 3 kms before Grover. By taking the Fish Creek Road, one is in the best position to hike, climb or fish in some of the best hiking and fishing areas of the Boulder. There's another road running up Pine Creek, passing the Aquarius Guard Station, and eventually ending at Chokecherry Point, but this is often rough and there's not a lot to see on top anyway.

Trail Information Since the Boulder Mountain is a very flat-topped plateau, it has not been used to a great extent for hiking or climbing. This is simply 4WD country and there are numerous 4WD type roads and tracks all over the top. As a result of the physical makeup of the land, hiking and most fishing has been confined to lakes and streams under the Rim. That's where most of the fishing lakes and maintained trails are found. In recent years with more interest in hiking, some 4WD tracks have been blocked off and trails built and maintained — especially between Lost Lake and Chokecherry Point. This is now a good hiking region, with many places where climbers can reach the rim top. The trails from Fish Creek to Beef Meadows and Chokecherry Point are the least used of all trails and hard to find.

Best Time and Time Needed Most of the lakes are around the 3100 meter level, while Boulter Top is between 3300 and 3400 meters. This means it's normally open by about mid-June and through October. Almost any hike in this area can be done in one day, but local scout groups enjoy overnight hikes and fishing trips.

Campgrounds There are several maintained campgrounds on Highway 12 between Torrey and Boulder, but none in this best hiking area. There is a fine camping site as shown on Spring Creek. Below the Rim there are springs and streams everywhere.

Maps Utah Travel Council Map 1 — Southeastern Utah, Dixie National Forest, U.S.G.S. maps Loa (1:100,000), Torrey, Grover (1:62,500), Loa 1 SE, Loa 4 NE (1:24,000)

Fish Ck. Lake right, on bench below the Boulder Top Escarpment (17mm lens).

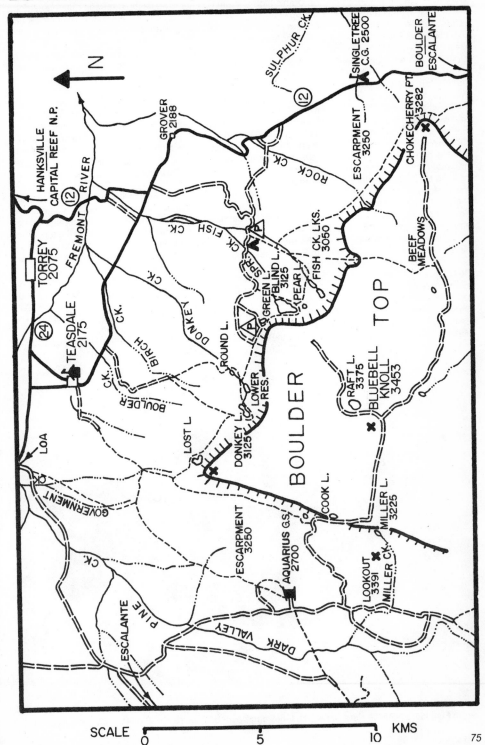

SCALE

0   5   10   KMS

31. Flat Top, Thousand Lake Mountain

Location Located in south-central Utah's high plateau country is an isolated mesa or plateau among the highest in the state. This is a flat top highland known as Thousand Lake Mountain. The highest part is 3446 meters, and on most maps this is known as the Flat Top. This area is immediately west of Capital Reef National Park, north of Bicknell and east of Loa.

Geology The part of Thousand Lake Mountain known as the Flat Top has been eroded away on all sides leaving an escarpment. The height varies from 50 to 75 vertical meters, but does not present a major obstacle to climbers. The very top is composed of various volcanic rocks. The entire area is heavily forested including the Flat Top.

Access One can approach the area from the east and Hanksville, or from the north or west from Richfield and Cedar City. The highway running from Loa to Torrey in the Fremont River Valley, south and west of the mountain, is US Highway 24. This is the same access as to Capital Reef National Park. For longer hikes, hikers can use dirt roads running into canyons from the areas of Fremont, Lyman, Bicknell, or Torrey. But the one and only road that takes people high on the mountain and to the Elkhorn Campground is the one running east from state road 72 and passing Heart Lake. This is a typical mountain road, rough in places, but generally maintained. This road reaches above 3000 meters and is open to traffic for only three or four months a year.

Trail Information If one is interested in getting to the top of Flat Top, but has little time, then drive to the Elkhorn C.G. If you have a passenger car it may be best to park there. The road going to Big Lake and beyond is, for the most part, a 4WD track. From the campground walk along the track for about 5 kms 'till you see a sign pointing out the Deep Creek — Flat Top Trail. Then simply follow this trail to the top. Since it's seldom used, pay attention to the markers on trees and small stone cairn. But for those wanting longer hikes it's possible to drive up Sand Creek from Torrey. Trail or Reese Creeks from near Lyman; or one could even use the Pole Canyon Trail to reach Elkhorn and the summit of Flat Top.

Best Time and Time Needed The hike from Elkhorn is a half day hike for most, but all day and two day hikes are possible from the lower canyons. Water is generally available in the lower canyons, but not on top. Hike from mid-June through October.

Campgrounds The Elkhorn Campground is a small but pleasant place and is free for camping. The Sunglow Campground is at a much lower elevation and may be crowded at times.

Maps Utah Travel Council Map 2 — Southeastern Central Utah, Fish Lake National Forest, U.S.G.S. maps Loa (1:100,000), Torrey (1:62,500), Loa 1 NE and SE (1:24,000)

From Fish Lake Hightop, one sees Fish Lake and beyond, Thousand Lake Mt. (105mm lens).

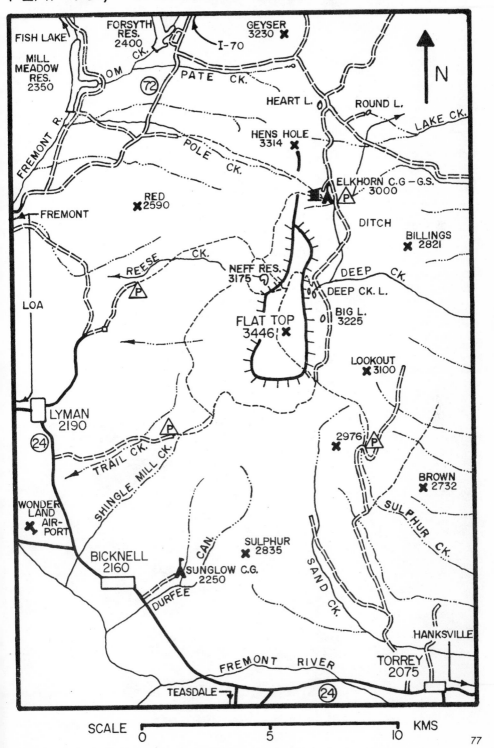

32. Fish Lake Hightop, Fish Lake Mountains

Location There are four major peaks or summits on this map, the highest of which is Fish Lake Hightop at 3546 meters. This is the big hulk of a mountain immediately to the northwest of Fish Lake, located north of Loa and southeast of Richfield in south-central Utah. The other three mountains are: Mt. Marvine, 3539 meters, by far the sharpest and most interesting peak to climb; Mt. Terrill, 3520 meters and just north of Marvine, which has a small solar-powered radio tower at the summit; and Mt. Hilgard, 3515 meters, the site of one of the minor Heliograph Stations dating from the 1880's.

Geology The most famous landmark of this area is Fish Lake. This Lake is actually in a graben, or down-faulted block, sandwiched inbetween Fish Lake Hightop and Mytoge Mountain. At one time the lake drained to the south, but later tilting caused it to drain northeast to Johnson Valley Reservoir and the Fremont River. The rocks are part of the Moroni Volcanic Series. Pelican Creek drainage is the path of a former glacier.

Access To climb Fish Lake Hightop, Marvine and Terrill, drive on Highway 24 to Fish Lake. From there drive up Sevenmile Creek to climb Marvine and Terrill. To climb Hilgard, either drive south from Interstate 70 on state road 72, or drive north out of Loa on the same graveled but well-used and well-maintained road.

Trail Information Here are the normal routes to each summit. Climb Fish Lake Hightop by driving or walking to Pelican Overlook, then use a popular and well-used trail running up Pelican Creek. Higher up, this trail turns into a 4WD track at times, and passes Tasha Spring. Then one can return by following Tasha Creek down to the water gauging station located on Sevenmile Creek. This is the best hike in the area. Mt. Marvine can be climbed from the west and Sevenmile Creek Road. No trail, just route-find up the west face. For Terrill, drive further up Sevenmile Creek and park near the guard station, then either walk cross country, or use an old 4WD track as shown on the map. The country here is open and easy to walk over. For Hilgard, make your way to Clear Creek G.S., then walk toward Willies Flat Reservoir, then north to the summit.

Best Time and Time Needed Each of the peaks can be climbed easily in one day, but Fish Lake Hightop can be made into an overnight hike. The hiking season is from about mid or late June through October in most years.

Campgrounds There are several campgrounds on the Fremont River and at Fish Lake. But Fish Lake is crowded, and it costs to camp. Drive to out of the way places for better camps.

Maps Utah Travel Council Map 6 — Southwestern Central Utah, Fishlake National Forest. U.S.G.S. maps Salina (1:100,000), Fish Lake, Mt. Terrill, Hilgard Mtn., Forsyth Reservoir (1:24,000).

Foto is from the top of Mt. Terrill, looking south at Mt. Marvine (105mm lens).

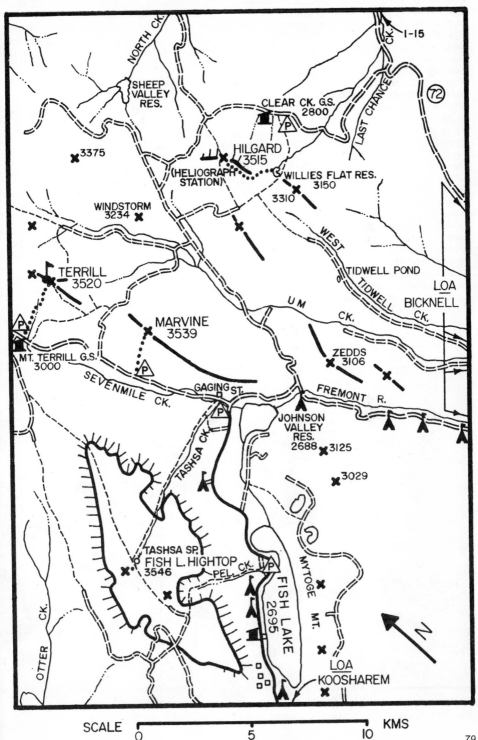

SCALE

0   5   10   KMS

33. Signal Peak, Sevier Plateau

Location The high summits and precipitous west faces shown on this map are part of the Sevier Plateau. This segment of plateau country is wedged in between the Pavant and Tushar Ranges to the west, and the Fishlake Hightop Mountain. It's due south of Richfield, and immediately east of Monroe. The highest point is Monroe Peak at 3422 meters. But this mountain will hardly be mentioned here because of a road and radio tower on top. The most interesting climb here is a fine hike to the summit of Glenwood Mountain, in which Signal Peak is the highest point at 3421 meters.

Geology Keep in mind this is a plateau with flat lying beds, but it's tilted down to the east, making a steep escarpment on the west face. The rock is tuff, ryolite, and basalt — all volcanic in origin.

Access Access to the main hiking area here is very good. There's a rather poor, but paved road up Monroe Canyon to a small recreation area known as Monrovian Park. This affords the best access for people with passenger cars and for those interested in hiking. There are many dirt and 4WD type roads higher on the plateau and on the eastern parts, but these places are not considered hiking areas. There's also a dirt or 4WD road from near the town of Annabella running to the southeast to a radio transmitter on the lower western ridge of Signal Peak, as shown on the map.

Trail Information To climb Signal Peak, this is probably the best route: Drive up Monroe Canyon and turn left up First Lefthand Fork. This is a steep, rough road, but high clearance vehicles can make it at least part way. After parking somewhere along the road, walk past the small hunters cabin, then along an old water pipeline to where the trail veers to the right. It then zig zags up the canyon wall on the south side, with many deer and sheep trails to make the way confusing. Eventually the trail meets the one running north-south as shown on the map. Walk north here crossing two fine streams. Later, the trail veers to the west and ends at the radio tower. Keep in mind the first objective is to reach the top of the prominent west ridge. Once one is on it, it's a scramble to the summit, through sagebrush, and a forest of aspen and pines.

Best Time and Time Needed The best time to hike here is from mid-June through October. If one uses the First Lefthand Fork route, expect to take most of one day. If the radio tower can be reached by car, the hike can be made in half a day.

Campgrounds Monrovian Park is more of a picnic area than a campground, but one can find many good campsites along First Lefthand Fork, with good running water.

Maps Utah Travel Council Map 6 — Southwestern Central Utah, Fishlake National Forest, U.S.G.S. maps Salina, Richfield (1:100,000), Monroe (1:62,500)

Foto shows Glenwood Mountains and rugged west face of Signal Peak (50mm lens).

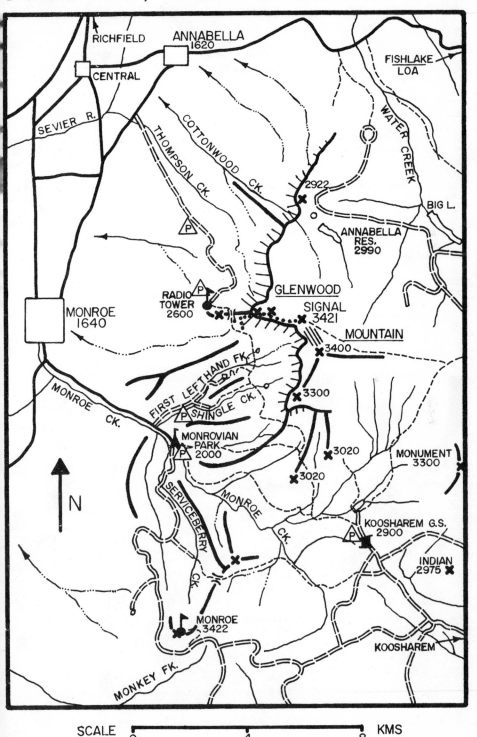

SCALE ⟼ KMS
0   4   8

34. Musinia Peak, Sevier Plateau

Location This map covers the mountain area directly east of the small town of Mayfield which is about 20 kms south of Manti in Sanpete County. These peaks are part of the Sevier Plateau which runs from near Interstate Highway 70 on the south to US Highway 6 and Soldier Summit on the north. The highest peak here is Heliotrope Mountain at 3393 meters. However, this is merely a long, flat ridge without much to interest climbers. The most interesting peak on the map is Musinia Peak at 3348 meters.

Geology This portion of the Sevier Plateau has three formations exposed. They are: Wasatch Formation on top, then the North Horn Formation, and generally at the lower levels, is the Mesaverde Group. Rocks are mostly limestone or sandstone.

Access There are dirt roads and 4WD tracks leading into this region from all directions, but the only easy way of reaching all of these summits is via Mayfield and the good gravel road running up Twelvemile Canyon. An alternative route would be to drive east out of Sterling (12 kms north of Mayfield) up Sixmile Canyon and into the area from the north on the Skyline Drive.

Trail Information Not many trails here, mostly 4WD tracks and of course some improved roads leading into the area. So it's likely you'll be walking over old 4WD tracks to near the peak you want to climb, then make the final ascent by simply route-finding. Keep in mind it's easy to walk through the forests here, with or without a trail. And the higher you climb, the more open the forest becomes. Timberline here is from about 3250 to 3350 meters. For Musinia, either walk or drive up Clear Creek or Beaver Creek to an area just west of the peak, then climb the west ridge. The east ridge can also be used. The north face is steeper. For Mt. Baldy, hike directly from Twelvemile Campground east of the peak. The same is true for a hike up Heliotrope Mountain. Climb it from the same campground. There are several summits around Island Lake, but they are of little interest to climbers.

Best Time and Time Needed All hikes in the area are considered day hikes. These are high mountains, so it's mid-June through October as the hiking season. There's lots of water throughout the area, but beware of the clay soil in the area of Musinia. When bad weather threatens, get out with your vehicle — at least from back country roads.

Campgrounds: There are several campgrounds around Ferron Reservoir with Twelvemile C.G. nearby and the Pinchot C.G. in Twelvemile Canyon. But one can camp anywhere.

Maps Utah Travel Council Maps 6 and 2, Southeastern Central Utah and Southwestern Central Utah, Manti-La Sal National Forest, U.S.G.S. maps, Manti (1:100,000), Sterling, Black Mtn., Ferron Reservoir, Mayfield, Woods Lake, Heliotrope Mtn. (1:24,000)

From Mayfield one can just see the pyramid of Musinia and its east ridge (105mm lens).

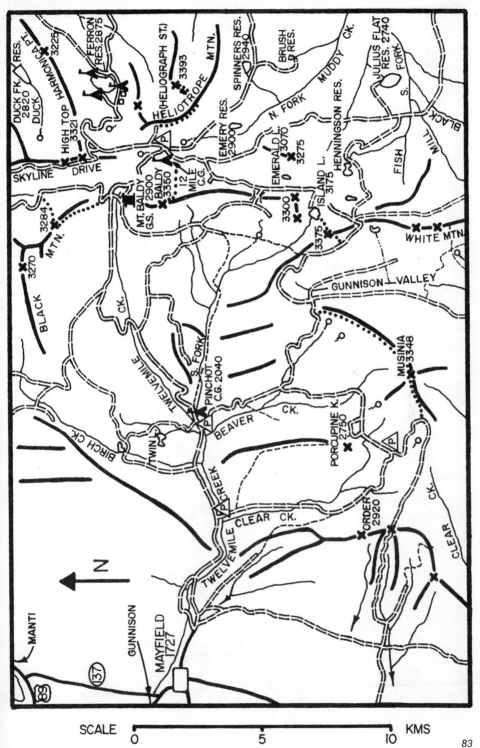

SCALE 0 — 5 — 10 KMS

35. South Tent Peak, Sevier Plateau

Location In the very heart of Utah, is one of the state's prime agricultural areas known as Sanpete Valley. And just to the east of this valley is the Wasatch Plateau, a high and wild hulk of a mountain mass forming a barrier to storm clouds, thus one of the state's best watershed areas. The highest point is South Tent Peak at 3440 meters. This particular section is directly east of Spring City.

Geology This area is not what geologists call true mountains, but is a massive plateau instead. The rock here was layed down in shallow seas, then uplifted, but at the same time remaining horizontal. Highest parts of the plateau are made up of the Flagstaff Formation. Under that is the North Horn Formation.

Access To reach the best hiking area one must use US Highway 89 running north-south in Sevier and Sanpete Valleys. At Spring City, drive east on 4th South Street to where it turns south, then simply follow it to Canal Canyon.

Trail Information Beware that this country is considered by many Utahn's as 4WD country, and the flat top nature of the plateau lends itself to that catagory. So there are very few maintained trails. What trails there are have usually been developed from old 4WD roads or tracks which originally were used to create water diversion systems, such as the ditches and one tunnel seen on the map. Also there are hunters' trails, used mostly in September and October. The trails shown on this map are unmaintained and difficult to locate in higher places. Drive to the mouth of Canal Canyon and to just above the bridge to where the cement ditches begin — at the diversion dam. Then cross the creek and locate the 4WD track on the other side. Once on this road follow it up Hell Hole Canyon where it turns into a trail higher up. This trail or one of the branching trails, takes hikers up to some cirque basins known as Little and Big Horsehoes. Again, these trails fade near the top so you may have to simply route-find to the rim top. Lots of water in this canyon. If it's South Tent Peak you want, drive further up Canal Canyon to where the road ends, then find the trail and follow it to where it too fades, then route-find to the rim top and follow the 4WD road east and eventually to the top of South Tent.

Best Time and Time Needed The hiking season here is from about mid-June on through October. From Canal Canyon to the top of Sanpete, West Sanpete or South Tent will take all day for most hikers. Some may want to camp in the canyon one night.

Campgrounds There are no developed campgrounds here, but everywhere is found good camping sites most of which have good water supplies.

Maps Utah Travel Council Map 2 — Southeastern Central Utah,Manti-La Sal National Forest, U.S.G.S. maps Manti (1:100,000), Spring City, South Tent Mtn. (1:24,000)

The Little Horseshoe and Canal Canyon as seen from above Spring City (105mm lens).

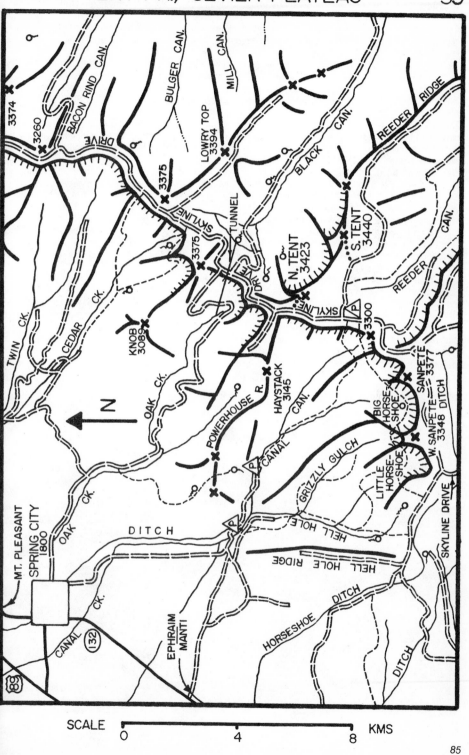

36. Mt. Agassiz, Uinta Mountains

Location This is the first of four maps covering the Uinta Mountains of Northeastern Utah. This one is the most westerly of the four. The entire mapped area is east of Kamas, Utah and south of Evanston, Wyoming. The highest summit here is Mt. Hayden at 3802 meters, but the best known peak, because of its proximity to Mirror Lake, is Mt. Agassiz, 3788 meters. Note the elevations of peaks. They get higher to the east.

Geology The Uinta Mountains run east-west and have been uplifted as are all true mountains. The central core of the range exposed at the higher elevations is a Precambian rock going by the name Uinta Mountain Group. It's entirely quartzite. Younger stratification is exposed around the perimeter of the range. During the last ice age the Uintas were heavily glaciated, leaving behind about 2000 small cirque lakes in dozens of basins.

Access During July and August, Mirror Lake is a popular place, mainly as a result of the building of Highway 150, running between Kamas and Evanston. From this one road, virtually all lakes and peaks can be reached. Other popular access roads are: up the Duchesne River to Defas Ranch, and the road along the Weber River to Holiday Park.

Trail Information: For Utahns this is the place everyone wants to take a week to do backpacking, hiking, climbing and fishing. The area has many trails, all of which are well-marked and well-used. It's recommended that a better map of the range, namely the Ashley and Wasatch National Forest map, be taken which shows many more lakes than this map. Bald Mountain is popular for climbing as there's a trail to the summit from Bald Mtn. Pass. Notch Peak can be climbed easily in about half a day from Trial Lake. A path goes right up into the notch to the other side. There's no trail to any other summit, but the forest is open and very easy to walk through even without a trail. Walk from Mirror Lake to about Scudder Lake, then route-find east to the top of Agassiz. For Hayden, drive to the pass north of Mirror Lake, then route-find east to the summit.

Best Time and Time Needed Bald Mtn. Pass is generally open by July 1, but the high country is generally wet at that time. Mid-July through mid-September is the hiking and fishing season. July has many mosquitos — take repellent. August brings heavy thunder showers — take a good tent and rain gear. A strong hiker could climb any peak near the highway in one day, but peaks along the eastern border of the map will require more time.

Campgrounds Note all the campgrounds on the map. This gives the reader an idea of the popularity of the region. Weekends in July, August and to mid-September are very crowded.

Maps Utah Travel Council Map 3 — Northeastern Central Utah, Ashley and Wasatch National Forests, U.S.G.S. maps Salt Lake City, Kings Peak (1:100,000)

A scene viewed by many: Mirror Lake, and to the east, Mt. Agassiz (50mm lens).

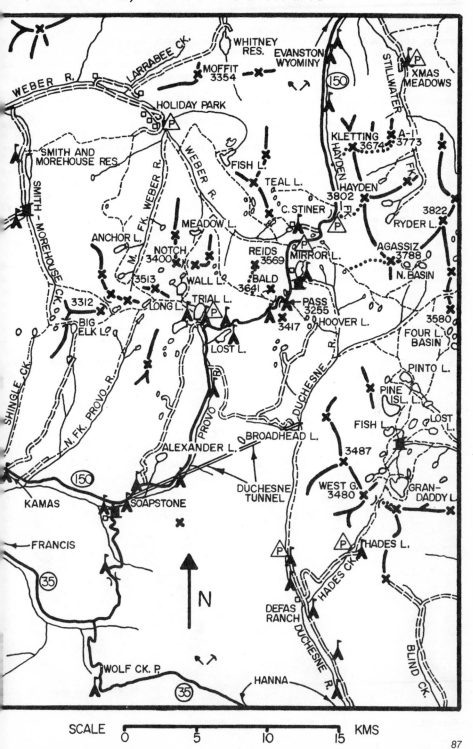

37. Mt. Lovenia, Uinta Mountains

Location This is the second of four maps covering the Uinta Mountains. Major drainages covered here are: Blacks Fork, Rock Creek and the Lake Fork River. Two of the twelve 4000 meter peaks in Utah are found on this map; Lovenia, 4032 and Tokewanna 4013 meters.

Geology The Uinta Mountains are the only major mountain range in the USA to run east-west, as opposed to north-south. These mountains have been uplifted at the same time as the rest of the Rocky Mountains, and are about the same height. The rocks at the higher elevations are all part of the Uinta Mountain Group, entirely quartzite. Around the edge of the range are various other rocks, all younger than those at the center of the range.

Access The main access roads are those up Lake Fork, Rock Creek and both the East and West Forks of Blacks Fork. But peaks such as Wilson can be reached from the Yellowstone River drainage; and Lamotte, Beulah and Yard can be reached best from the East Fork of the Bear River. If going into Blacks Fork, first go to Mountain View and Robertson in Wyoming, then follow the signs south up Blacks Fork. If heading for south slope routes, go first to Duchesne and Mountain Home, then follow signs to Rock or Lake Fork Creeks.

Trail Information The most popular activity here is fishing, so it's important to have one of the forest service maps which better lists the lakes than this one. The signs along the way always list lakes as destinations, not peaks. All trails are well-used and maintained, and well-signposted. To climb Lovenia, a north slope route would be shorter — namely from East Fork of Blacks Fork. Climb Red Castle and Wilson also from East Fork of Blacks Fork, or possibly East Fork of Smiths Fork. Cleveland and Explorer Peaks can both be climbed from Ottoson Basin, up from Moon Lake, or from the East Fork of Rock Creek and Squaw Basin. There are no trails to the tops of any mountains here, but most climbs are easy. Timberline here is about 3350 meters.

Best Time and Time Needed This map shows some of the highest peaks and lakes in the Uinta Mountains, so don't expect to find dry conditions until about the first week of July, and often times not until mid-July. Labor Day weekend is about the end of the season for most people, but good weather is normal for September. Climbing Lovenia would be three easy days from the north, or 3 long days or more from Moon Lake. Cleveland and Explorer Peaks about three days from Moon Lake.

Campgrounds Expect to find Moon Lake crowded on weekends, as would be the case with any developed recreation site, but other areas are not as popular. There are several campgrounds on the map, but camping sites are found everywhere.

Maps Utah Travel Council Map 3 — Northeastern Central Utah, Wasatch and Ashley National Forests, U.S.G.S. maps Kings Peak, Duchesne (1:100,000)

From Mt. Powell, one sees the north face of Red Castle Peak (50mm lens).

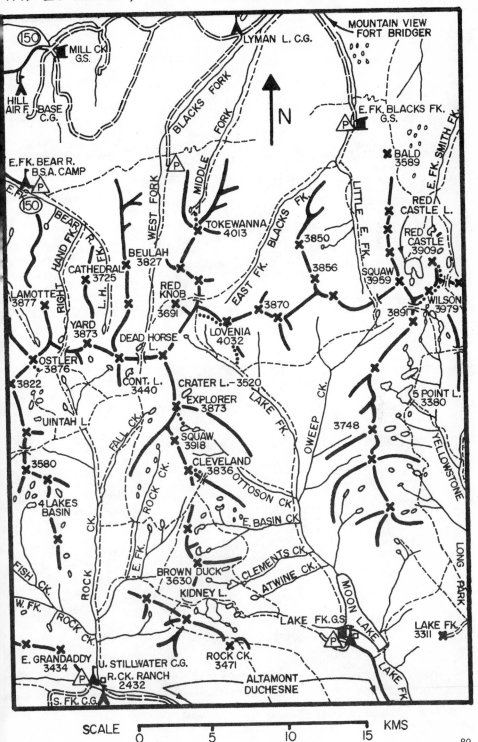

From Hayden Peak, Highway 150, Mirror Lake, Bald Mt., Reids Peak (50mm lens).

Typical campsite in the High Uintas Primitive Area (50mn lens).

Lake Atwood in the upper Uinta River is one of the best fishing lakes (50mm lens).

This is a winter scene showing north face of Henry's Fork Peak and Henry's Fork Basin (50mm lens).

Early winter in the Uintas. Wilson Pk. far right, 5 Point Lake left (50mm lens).

Looking northeast across upper Swift Creek drainage at Mt. Emmons (50mm lens).

This is the trailhead at Henry's Fork Campground, Henry's Fork Creek (50mm lens).

Most streams in the Uintas are bridged, but not here on the upper Uinta River (50mm lens).

38. Kings Peak, Uinta Mountains

Location On this map are ten of the twelve 4000 meter peaks in the state. This is the very heart of the Uintas with thes highest peak in Utah, Kings Peak, 4123 meters. Second highest is Gilbert Peak at 4097 meters, and third, Mt. Emmons, 4096 meters. The names of two summits have been named by this author, Henry's Fork Peak and Gunsight Peak. They are unnamed on USGS maps. This part of the Uintas is northwest of Neola, north of Altamont, and due south of Ft. Bridger and Mountain View in Wyoming.

Geology The Uintas are a huge uplifted range, with Precambrian quartzite rocks exposed at higher elevations and in the center of the range. Around the perimeter are found various other kinds of rocks, all tilting away from the mountains.

Access From the north one can approach this region by driving to Mountain View, Wyoming, then turn south and drive up Henry's Fork, or Smiths Fork to China Meadows. Take a Utah and Wyoming state highway map for this part of your trip. Roads are well-signposted to these two places. From the south, one must first proceed to Neola, then drive north into the Uinta River Canyon; or go to Altamont and then to the Yellowstone River Drainage.

Trail Information Again, take along a map of the Wasatch or Ashley National Forest because signposts along the trails nearly always point out the way to lakes, never mountains. The trails in the Uintas are well-used and well-maintained by the forest service. Trails are marked by cuts on trees, and above timberline (3350 meters) by small stone cairns. No problem finding trails here. To climb Kings Peak, the easiest and shortest route is to drive to the Henry's Fork Trailhead and Campground on the north slope. From there walk up to Henry's Fork Basin, Gunsight Pass, Anderson Pass and then south up the north ridge to the summit. Gilbert Peak is also best climbed from Henry's Fork. One can also hike up Yellowstone or Uinta Rivers to Anderson Pass, but these are longer routes. One can even walk up Swift Creek, then use the long south ridge of Kings Peak to reach the highest point. Mt. Emmons can best be climbed from Swift Creek, with the Uinta River and the U-Bar Ranch the second best route. Climb the Burros Peaks from Hoop Lake.

Best Time and Time Needed Climb here from about the first week in July on through mid-September. Nights are cold in September, though. From Henry's Fork it's about 3 easy days to climb Kings Peak, but 3 long days from Yellowstone River and maybe 3 or 4 days by using the Uinta River route.

Campgrounds The campgrounds in the major drainages are becoming more popular each year, but they are not nearly as crowded as places such as Mirror Lake and vicinity.

Maps Utah Travel Council Map 3 — Northeastern Central Utah, Wasatch and Ashley National Forests, U.S.G.S. maps Kings Peak, Duchesne (1:100,000)

From Mt. Powell, looking east across Henry's Fork Basin towards Gilbert Peak (50mm lens).

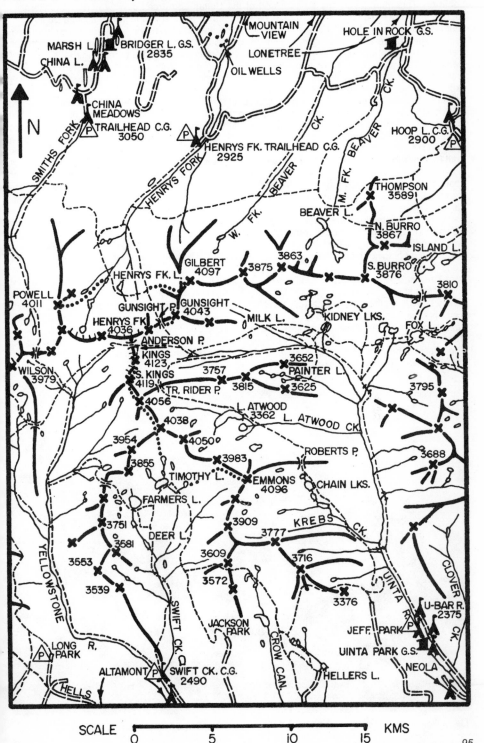

39. Marsh Peak, Uinta Mountains

Location This map covers the eastern end of the Uintas and areas directly north of Whiterocks, Lapoint and Tridell. The better known peak here, and the one most visible from the Uinta Basin to the south is Marsh Peak at 3731 meters. Nowhere to the east of Marsh and Leidy Peaks are there any peaks rising above timberline. This part of the Uintas is much more flat than the central portions, therefore we see many more parks or meadows, and many more logging areas with roads.

Geology The geologic cross section, shown on another page, runs through the eastern part of this area. It shows quartzite rocks in the center of the range, with progressively younger rocks being exposed at the outer edges of this anticline, or dome shaped structure.

Access If it's the Whiterocks River you're interested in reaching, drive to the settlement of Whiterocks north of Roosevelt. From there, follow the signs north to the Whiterocks Campground, or to Pole Lake, and beyond. Paradise Park and campground is another popular place which is reached from Lapoint. Drive northwest out of Vernal and up either Dry Fork or Ashley Creek to reach the areas just east of Leidy and Marsh Peaks. On the north slopes drive to either Browne or Spirit Lake and hike from there.

Trail Information The quickest way to reach Marsh Peak is to drive up Dry Fork out of Vernal, then along Brownie Creek to Ashley Twin Lakes. Then either look for a trail running to the south of Marsh Peak, or simply route-find up the east face. Marsh can be climbed from Paradise Park, too. Take the hard-to-find trail out of the campground, or use the road running into Dry Fork Canyon from near Paradise. There's a maze of old logging roads here, but look for stone cairns and routes to the Mosby Canal. A trail exists along the canal, which eventually intersects the main trail running east towards Marsh Peak. Once near the peak route-find up the west face. Climb Leidy from Brown Lake, Ashley Twin Lakes, or Long Park at the head of the North Fork of Ashley Creek. Climb Chepeta from Spirit Lake or the road running north from Pole Lake. Trails in this part of the Uintas are well marked, most of which are fairly well used.

Best Time and Time Needed The hiking season here is the same as for the rest of the Uintas; July, August and to mid-September. The author climbed Marsh in one long day from Paradise Park. From Ashley Twin Lakes it's a short day hike. Leidy Peak from Long Park Reservoir, a short day hike. Chepeta from Spirit Lake is also an easy day trip.

Campgrounds There are fine campgrounds at Pole and Spirit Lakes and at Paradise Park.

Maps Utah Travel Council Map 3 — Northeastern Central Utah, Ashley National Forest, U.S.G.S. maps Dutch John, Kings Peak (1,100,000), Chepeta Lake, Whiterocks Lake, Leidy Peak, Marsh Peak, Paradise Park, Rasmussen Lakes (1:24,000)

Liedy Peak in the eastern Uintas. Seen from the east and Trout Peak (105mm lens).

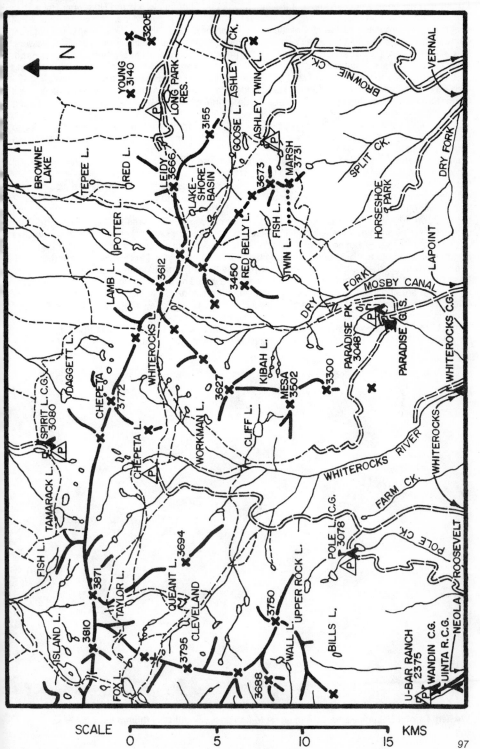

40. Patmos Head, Book Cliffs

Location Few people in Utah know of the mountains and plateaus in eastern Utah near Price. The highest area is east and north of Dragerton, East Carbon City and Sunnyside. These are three small coal mining communities at the foot of the Book, Roan or Brown Cliffs. Various maps use different names. The highest summit is Bruin Point at 3135 meters. On top of this flat summit are radio towers. Next highest is Mt. Bartles at 3063 meters. But the peak of most interest to climbers is Patmos Head, rising to 3003 meters. Patmos Head has steep escarpments on all sides except for the ridge running north. On top are the remains of an old Heliograph Station dating from the 1880's.

Geology At the very summit of Patmos Head is the Green River Formation. Next is the Wasatch and North Horn Formations, followed by the Mesa Verde Group. It's in the Mesa Verde that the coal is being mined at the Geneva and Sunnyside Mines.

Access Drive southeast out of Price on US Highway 6, then directly east on State Road 123 running to East Carbon City. There are paved roads to the Geneva and Sunnyside mines. On the map, most trails shown are actually 4WD roads.

Trail Information This is not one of the popular weekend hiking areas in Utah; therefore, no trail system exists. But there are plenty of 4WD tracks. There's a road to the top of both Bruin Point and Mt. Bartles, but not to Patmos Head. So it's Patmos that'll be discussed here. If you have a nice car and don't like driving on rough, dusty roads, stop at the Geneva Mine and walk from there. Or drive about 2 kms further up the canyon and stop at a side road just above the water tanks. Walk along the canyon bottom north, sometimes on a 4WD road. Turn right in a canyon west of the summit and either go up that canyon, or up the prominent west ridge. There are easy grass and pine forest covered slopes, as well as a few cliffs to be skirted, but no major problems. Take all your own water, there's none in the canyons. Regular hiking boots are best here. Patmos Head can also be climbed from Range Creek (but you'll need a 4WD to get there), from Number 2 Canyon and along Patmos Mountain Ridge.

Best Time and Time Needed Best time for hiking here would be June, September and October. July and August are fine too, but a little warm. Because of the steepness of the climb and the fact no trail exists, it will take an entire day for this climb for the average hiker. For a strong hiker, about half a day. Excellent views from the top of much of Utah's canyon and cliff country.

Maps Utah Travel Council Map 2 — Southeastern Central Utah, U.S.G.S. maps Price, Huntington (1:100,000), Woodside (1:62,500), Patmos Head, Bruin Point, Mt. Bartles, Sunnyside (1:24,000)

Western face of Patmos Head. One must route-find past several cliffs (35mm lens).

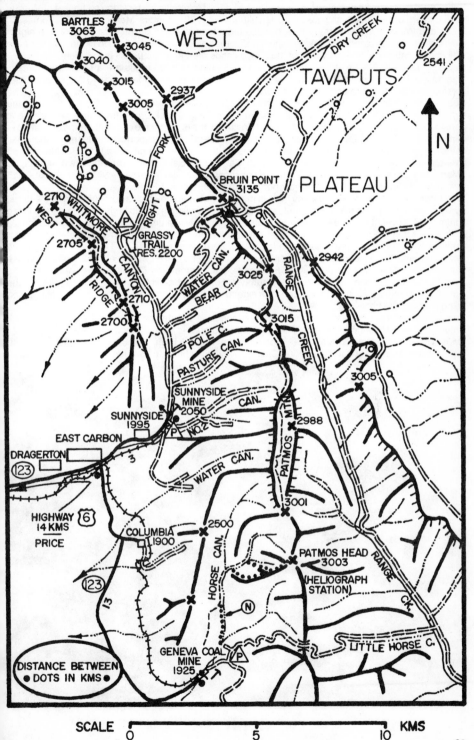

PATMOS HEAD, BOOK CLIFFS

BARTLES 3063
3045
3040
3015
3005
2937
WEST
DRY CREEK
2541
TAVAPUTS
N
BRUIN POINT 3135
PLATEAU
2710 WHITMORE
WEST
RIGHT FORK
P
GRASSY TRAIL RES. 2200
2705
CANYON
RIDGE
WATER CAN.
BEAR C.
3025
RANGE
2942
2710
2700
POLE C.
PASTURE CAN.
3015
CREEK
3005
SUNNYSIDE MINE 2050
CAN.
SUNNYSIDE 1995
P NO.2
2988
PATMOS MTN.
EAST CARBON
DRAGERTON
123
3
WATER CAN.
3001
HIGHWAY 14 KMS
6
PRICE
COLUMBIA 1900
2500
123
13
HORSE CAN.
N
PATMOS HEAD 3003
(HELIOGRAPH STATION)
RANGE
CK.
DISTANCE BETWEEN
● DOTS IN KMS ●
GENEVA COAL MINE 1925
P
LITTLE HORSE C.

SCALE
0   5   10
KMS

41. Mt. Peale, La Sal Mountains

Location Mt. Peale, 3878 meters, is located in the La Sal Mountains not far to the southeast of Moab in southeastern Utah. Other high peaks include Tukuhnikivatz, 3806 meters; Mellenthin, 3855; Tomasaki, 3729; and Waas, 3759 meters. Although these mountains are in a desert environment, the higher elevations have fine stands of quaking aspen, ponderosa pine, spruce and fir. The highest portions are well above timberline, and the views of the canyonlands area from the peaks is excellent.

Geology Like the Abajos, the Henrys and Navajo Mountains, the LaSals are a laccolith mountain. Magma was forced from within the earth through the crust, but frozen before reaching the surface. Later erosion exposed the core and the diorite porphyry.

Access The main access road is one which turns in an easterly direction from Highway 163 near the Grand County Airport southeast of Moab. This road first follows Pack Creek, then turns northeast and parallels Brumley Creek. This road runs toward Castleton, but most people will want to stop and camp at either Oowah or Warner Lakes. Camping at either of these lakes gives good access to the northern half of the range. To climb Peale and other peaks in the south part of the range, drive to La Sal Junction, 35 kms south of Moab. From there go east to La Sal and La Sal Creek. From the main highway to 1Medicine Lake is a very rough road, but most passenger cars can make it — with care. About 4 or 5 kms short of Medicine Lake, simply walk north up the south face of Peale.

Trail Information There are few if any trails in the La Sal Mountains which are maintained by the forest service. There are some old mining roads and trails used by cattlemen and hunters, but no trails to the summits. However, it's very easy to simply walk through the forest until timberline is reached, then it's even easier. On the map one can see the best hiking routes to some of the higher peaks. All major canyons have springs or streams, as this is a well-watered highland area.

Best Time and Time Needed From near Medicine Lake, one could climb Peale in 2-3 hours, or take half a day for Peale and Tukuhnikivatz. For peaks near Warner and Oowah Lakes about the same amount of time is needed, depending on the number of peaks to be climbed. Heavy snows will block the higher roads until early June. The season then extends from June through October, with the fall season being perhaps the best.

Campgrounds There are forest service campgrounds at Warner and Oowah Lakes and at Pack Creek, but one can camp anywhere. The least crowded area is around Medicine Lake.

Maps Utah Travel Council Map 2 — Southeastern Central Utah, Manti-La Sal National Forest, U.S.G.S. maps Moab, La Sal (1:100,000), Castle Valley, Polar Mesa, La Sal Junction, La Sal(1:62,500)

Looking west from Mt. Peale, one sees the top of Tukuhnikivatz along a ridge (50mm lens).

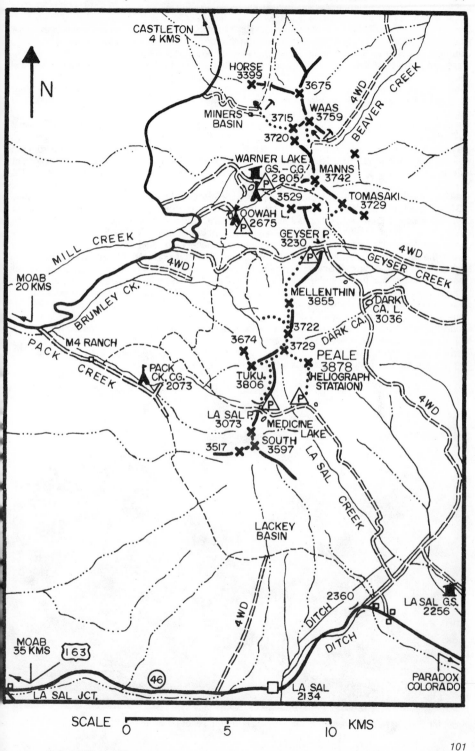

42. Mt. Ellen, Henry Mountains

Location The Henry Mountains are located in southeastern Utah, almost due south of Hanksville. The range protrudes from the Colorado Plateau which is rather flat and at low altitude, therefore the area is very dry and isolated. A herd of buffalo roam the foothills of the Henrys and is the only place in the USA where wild buffalo are hunted. The highest peak in the range is Mt. Ellen at 3512 meters.

Geology The Henrys, like the Abajo, La Sal and Navajo Mountains, is a laccolith, formed by a moulton mass of magma from within the earth trying to reach the surface. Instead of reaching the surface and becoming a volcano, it merely deformed the surface rock strata and froze in place. Later erosion removed the overlaying rocks, leaving the core exposed. See the geologic cross section for the Henry Mountains. The rock high on the mountain is diorite porphyry. Many mines exist on the eastern side of the range.

Access By far the better way to reach the Henrys is to drive south out of Hanksville on the Sawmill Basin Road, in the direction of Lonesome Beaver Campground. If coming from Hite on Lake Powell, use the eastern approach passing Lone Cedar and follow Crescent Creek. You can also get there from the west and Capital Reef N.P. (the Notom-Bullfrog Road). Check at the BLM office in Hanksville for current road conditions. The road from near Burtons Peak to Lonesome Beaver C.G. was impassable for 4WDs in 1982.

Trail Information No real trails here, but a lot of 4WDX TRACKS LEADING UP TO OLD, AND SOME NOT SO OLD, MINES. With the dry climate, the higher south facing slopes are completely grass covered, while the north-facing slopes have aspen, fir and spruce forests. Traveling cross-country is easy with or without a trail. Here are some normal routes to the summits. Climb Ellen Peak from the Lonesome Beaver Campground. Simply walk up the east face. One could also walk up the road to the pass to the south, then north along the north-south ridge. The south end of Mt. Ellen can be climbed from Lonesome Beaver, or from Bromide Basin (from which Crescent Creek flows) on the east. To climb Pennell, drive into the area from the Trachyte Ranch. Only the head waters of Crescent, Slate and Bull Creeks have reliable water. These are year-round flowing streams. Carry some water in your car.

Best Time and Time Needed Any time from late May through October is a good time to visit the Henrys. Any of these climbs can be done in one day.

Campgrounds Campsites are everywhere, but campgrounds are only at Lonesome Beaver, and at McMillan Springs on the west side of the range.

Maps Utah Travel Council Map 1 — Southeastern Utah, U.S.G.S. maps Hite Crossing, Hanksville (1:100,000), Mt. Ellen, Mt. Pennell, Bull Mtn., Mt. Hillers (1:62,500)

From Mt. Ellens; Bartons Peak left, Mt. Pennell right, Mt. Hiller far away (105mm lens).

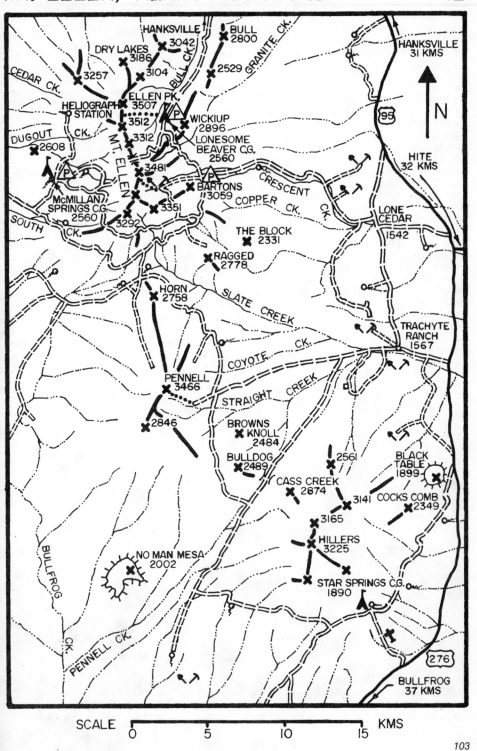

HANKSVILLE 3042
BULL 2800
DRY LAKES 3186
CEDAR CK.
3257
3104
2529
GRANITE CK.
BULL CK.
HANKSVILLE 31 KMS
95
N
ELLEN PK. 3507
HELIOGRAPH STATION 3512
WICKIUP 2896
LONESOME BEAVER C.G. 2560
3312
DUGOUT CK.
2608
MT. ELLEN
3481
HITE 32 KMS
P
BARTONS 3059
CRESCENT CK.
McMILLAN SPRINGS C.G. 2560
3351
COPPER CK.
LONE CEDAR 1542
SOUTH CK.
3292
THE BLOCK 2331
RAGGED 2778
HORN 2758
SLATE CREEK
TRACHYTE RANCH 1567
COYOTE CK.
PENNELL 3466
STRAIGHT CREEK
2846
BROWNS KNOLL 2484
BULLDOG 2489
2561
BLACK TABLE 1899
CASS CREEK 2874
3141
COCKS COMB 2349
3165
HILLERS 3225
BULLFROG CK.
NO MAN MESA 2002
STAR SPRINGS C.G. 1890
276
PENNELL CK.
BULLFROG 37 KMS

SCALE
0   5   10   15   KMS

43. Abajo Peak, Abajo Mountains

Location The Abajo Mountains are located in the extreme southeastern corner of Utah just west of Monticello. This range has a number of summits over 3000 meters, the highest of which is Abajo Peak at 3463 meters. On the northeastern slopes of Abajo Peak is the Blue Mountain Ski Resort. It's the only place to ski in southeastern Utah. Abajo Peak is forested right up to the summit. The higher south-facing slopes are grass covered, while the north-facing slopes are covered with spruce, fir and aspen trees. Logging is a minor local industry. On top of Abajo Peak is a radio tower. During summer months good 4WD vehicles can make it to the summit, but there are many good hiking routes to the top as well.

Geology The Abajo Mountains have been made the same as the La Sals, Henrys, and Navajo Mountains. They are known as laccolith mountains. Moulton magma was forced up through cracks in the earth, but failed to reach the surface. But it did deform or push up other formations. Later erosion left the intrusive body exposed.

Access By far the best all around route to reach the higher summits of the Abajo is the paved road running west out of Monticello. It's paved for about 10 kms, to the Buckboard Campground. Higher up, this road is steep, but good up to the Indian Creek Guard Station. One can also reach the area via the Natural Bridges N.M. on the south side of the range and from various other roads, but they are generally less well maintained.

Trail Information Because of the nature of the topography and vegetation, there are very few if any backpacking trails in the Abajos. Instead it's mostly 4WD tracks one encounters. Even with these setbacks, hiking and climbing can still be enjoyed. To climb Abajo Peak, the least complicated way would be to drive to the Blue Mountain Ski Resort, then simply follow the lifts to the top of the main north-south summit ridge, thence south to the summit. A second choice would be to drive to the pass between Abajo and Horsehead Peaks and climb from there. This pass is the best route to use to climb Horsehead as well. From near this same pass, The Twins and North Peaks can also be climbed. Plenty of small streams and water in the canyons.

Best Time and Time Needed: All peaks in the Abajos are one day climbs. The hiking season is from about June 1 through October, and in some years into November.

Campgrounds Both Buckboard and Dalton Spring Campgrounds are fee-use areas, but good campsites are everywhere around the high peaks.

Maps Utah Travel Council Map 1 — Southeastern Utah, Manti-La Sal National Forest, U.S.G.S. maps Blanding (1:100,000), Monticello, Mt. Linnaeua (1:62,500)

Horsehead Mountain (southeast slopes) as seen from the summit of Abajo Peak (35mm lens).

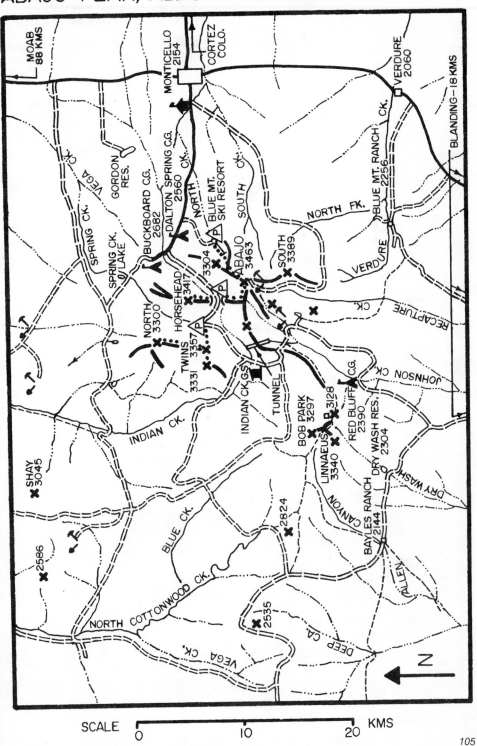

SCALE

0   10   20   KMS

44. Navajo Mountain — Rainbow Bridge

Location Navajo Mountain and Rainbow Bridge National Monument are on this map. Both of these natural features are in extreme southern Utah very near the Utah-Arizona state line. Navajo Mountain rises to 3166 meters.

Geology Navajo Mountain is one of 8 mountains on the Colorado Plateau which are known as laccolith mountains. The flat-lying rocks of the Colorado Plateau were pushed up by molten magma from below. As the magma neared the surface, it cooled and became a vertical column. Later erosion will expose this central core, but as yet it is still beneath the sandstone making up the plateau. Rainbow Bridge is made of Navajo Sandstone.

Access For most Utahns the fastest way to get there is to drive to Kanab, then to Page, Arizona, and east on Highway 98 about 83 kms to the road leading to Inscription House Trading Post, and eventually to Navajo Mtn.town, where is located a mission school, church and store-gas station complex. It's about 66 kms of gravel and sandy roads from the paved highway to the town of Navajo Mtn. Another way of getting to the area is via Blanding, Mexican Hat, and Kayenta. Most visitors to the Rainbow Bridge are now coming in by boat from Lake Powell.

Trail Information To climb Navajo Mountain, drive to its base by using the first road south of Navajo Mtn. town, going towards the mountain. Park just before the steep and rough part and walk on the road all the way to the top, or route-find through the forest. On top is a radio-television transmitter. There are two trails to Rainbow Bridge. The best trail is the one beginning at the abandoned Rainbow Lodge — this is the old route to the bridge before Lake Powell. The other trail begins at Cha Canyon. Use light weight leather or canvas hiking boots, or even the new running shoes. Sandy trails all the way.

Best Time and Time Needed The best hiking time for the mountain is in early summer and early fall. For the bridge hike, spring and fall are best, with summer being very warm and winters cold. Climbing the mountain is a one-day hike, while the bridge hike is one day in and one day out — the same way. Unfit hikers may want 3 days. Making a loop from the Rainbow Lodge to Cha Canyon will be two or three days, but then one must have two vehicles for this trip.

Campgrounds Camping is best of course, at or near springs as shown on the map. Echo Camp near the bridge is the closest thing to a real campground. At the time of your arrival, stop at Navajo Mtn. town and make inquiries as to the present conditions and location of water. Some should be carried at all times.

Maps U.S.G.S. maps Navajo Mtn. (1:100,000), Navajo Mtn. (1:62,500) in Utah, and Chaiyahi Flat, Chaiyahi Rim NE (1:24,000) both in Arizona.

Navajo Mountain from the southeast. Route is up center-most canyon (50mm lens).

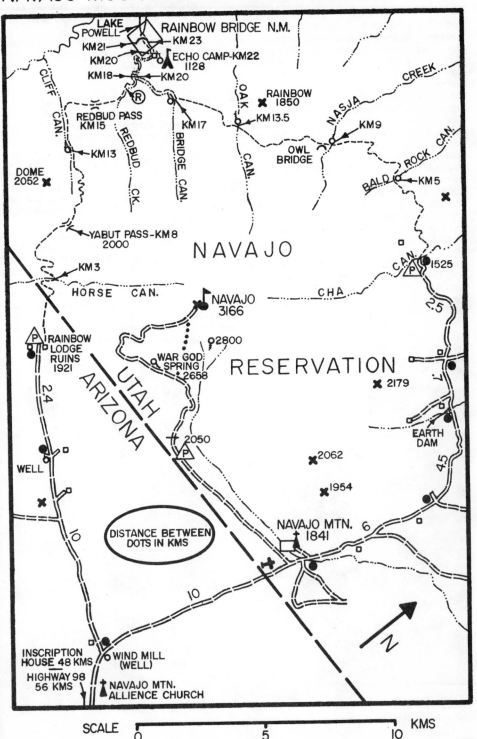

SCALE |0————————5————————10| KMS

45. Zion Narrows, Zion National Park

Location This map shows much of the eastern portion of Zion National Park and includes Zion Canyon. Zion is located in extreme southwestern Utah between St. George, Mt. Carmel Junction, and Cedar City. Here is one of Utah's best canyon hikes, Zion Narrows.

Geology The small geologic cross section on the map explains it best. Capping much of Zions buttes and mesas, is the Carmel Formation. It's a mixture of limestone and sandstone. The Navajo Sandstone is the layer which forms the narrow canyon walls of the Zion Narrows. Below the Narrows and as the canyon widens, is the Keyenta Formation.

Access Access to Zion Canyon is easy. One can drive east out of St. George and through the small towns of Hurricane, La Verkin, Virgin and Springdale, or west from Mt. Carmel Junction located on US Highway 89. The road running north into Zion Canyon gives access to the bottom end of the Narrows Hike and is open year-round. To reach the upper end of the canyon, and the starting point for the hike, drive east out of the park about 3 kms, then turn north on a gravel road for 29 kms to the Chamberlain Ranch.

Trail Information The Zion Narrows Hike has no trail — you simply walk down the canyon. About one quarter of the time is spent walking in the Virgin River. There is a short paved trail up-canyon from Temple of Siva for about 1½ kms. Many people park at the end-of-road parking lot and walk upstream into the narrows, then return the same way. But for the whole adventure, the trip is begun at the Chamberlain Ranch. The first part is on a 4WD road, then the river bottom. The real narrows begin 2 kms above a waterfall, and end not far above the Temple of Siva. The narrowest part is downstream from Big Spring to near the paved trail. Ideal footwear is a canvas boot, but most people use running shoes. The slippery, algae-covered rocks make walking slightly difficult. From Chamberlain's Ranch to Siva is about 20 kms. Occasional deep pools make it impossible for small children to make this hike. Residents of Springdale run car shuttle services.

Best Time and Time Needed Because of heavy spring runoff and the cold waters, late June is the beginning of the hiking season. This runs to late September. Be aware of thunderstorms and flash floods in late July and August. Always consult park rangers at the visitor center about weather, road conditions, etc., before entering the canyon. Easy day hikes can begin and end at Temple of Siva. Chamberlain's Ranch to Siva is a long day-hike. If you're doing the entire 20 kms hike, and want to really enjoy it, take two full days. Take extra dry clothing if camping in the canyon — these cold waters and shaded canyon reduce body temps.

Campgrounds Overnighting is permitted in the Narrows, but not below Big Spring.

Maps U.S.G.S. maps Kanab (1:100,000), Zion National Park (1:31,680)

The narrowest of The Narrows in the Zion Narrows. It's near hip deep in places (17mm lens).

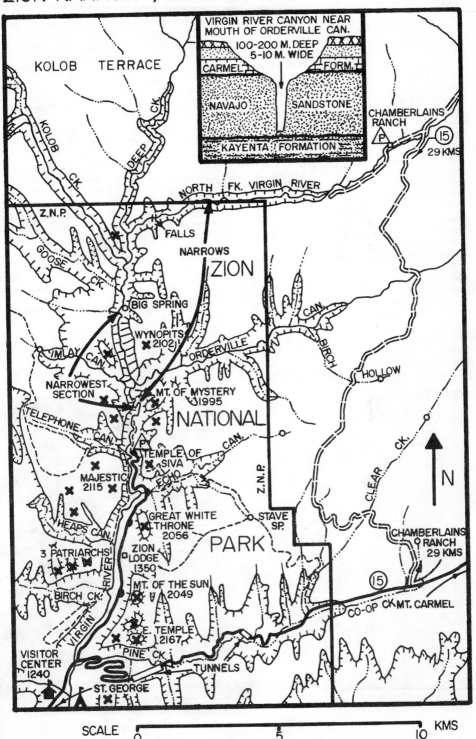

46. Paria River — Buckskin Gulch

Location One of the best known Utah canyon hikes is the Paria River and its largest tributary, the Buckskin Gulch. One has to drive only about 3 kms off US Highway 89, which runs between Kanab, Utah and Page, Arizona, to be at the trailhead. This hike is half in Utah, half in Arizona. End of hike is at Lees Ferry. The narrows of Paria is about 8 kms long, and 7 or 8 meters wide on the average, with the narrowest part 3 to 4 meters. The Buckskin Gulch averages 4 meters in width for 20 kms, with the narrowest part one meter. Depth of both is about 125 meters.

Geology The geologic cross section tells the story. It's the Navajo Sandstone that makes the narrow canyons. Downstream the river cuts into the Kayenta and Moenave Formations.

Access Always start at the Paria River R.S. on Highway 89, 58 kms east of Kanab, to get the latest word on weather, additional maps and information on the water situation. Then drive to the trailhead, 3 kms. If entering the Buckskin, use the House Rock Valley Road which begins about 8 kms west of the Paria River R.S. on Highway 89. This road is rough, but most cars can make it to KM 0, about 6 kms from the highway.

Trail Information There are no trails here, just walk in or along the stream. The Paria's flow depends on up-stream irrigation, but it's a flowing stream most of the year. The Buckskin is dry, with very few springs. Since you walk in water much of the time, the best footwear is a canvas boot, but many use a running shoe. The water in Paria is less than ankle deep with boy scout groups doing the hike regularly. If one is to walk from Whitehouse to Lee's Ferry, a car shuttle is needed. There are people at Marble Canyon who run shuttle services. But one could walk down the Buckskin, up the Paria, then walk, hitch-hike or bum a ride back to one's car on the House Rock Road. Buckskin is the more interesting of the two canyons.

Best Time and Time Needed The hike from Whitehouse to Lee's Ferry is 3 days or longer, depending on side trips. Distance is 56 kms. If doing the Buckskin to Lee's Ferry expect about one day longer to walk 72 kms. If doing the Buckskin to the Whitehouse, plan on 2 or 3 days. If doing the Buckskin, take along a 10 meter long rope to make a safe descent in the rock jam at KM 24.2. Hike during April, May, June, September, October and November. Paria River water needs to be treated or boiled. August brings rain, flash flooding, and danger, especially to the Buckskin.

Campgrounds There are campgrounds at both ends of the hike, and many campsites inbetween. Take several water bottles to fill if camping in places without water. Always camp on higher ground. Take a backpacker's stove, as wood is becoming scarce.

Maps Utah Travel Council Map 5, U.S.G.S. maps Smokey Mtn. (1:100,000), Paria (Utah), Paria Plateau and Lee's Ferry (Arizona) (1:62,500), B.L.M. "Paria Canyon Primitive Area."

Best part of the Paria River Hike is the Buckskin Gulch seen here (17mm lens).

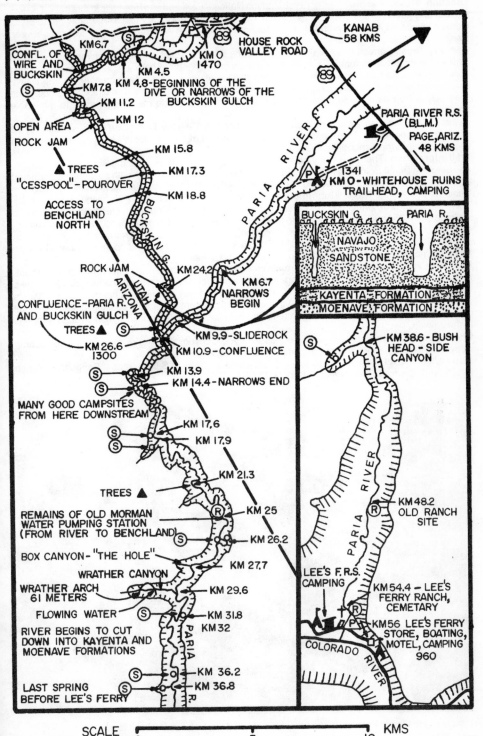

SCALE
0   5   10   KMS

47. Bryce Canyon National Park

Location This map shows most of Bryce Canyon National Park and all of the trails in that park. The trail of most emphasis here is the Under-The-Rim Trail running from Bryce Point to Rainbow Point. Bryce Canyon is located in southcentral Utah not far north of the Utah-Arizona state line. It lies in between Panguitch, Tropic and Kanab.

Geology Bryce Canyon is not really a canyon, but a series of small, short side canyons which form a series of amphitheaters running in a north-south direction. We have here a high and almost flat plain called the Paunsagunt Plateau. At the eastern edge erosion is taking place creating an impressive escarpment with thousands of pinnacles and spires all colored a bright pink. The pink color is due to the presence of iron particles in the rock which oxidize and impart the resulting pigment to the whole formation.

Access Only one road leads to the park and it dead ends at Rainbow Point. One must use Highway 12 which links Panguitch to Tropic and Escalante. In the winter of 1982-83 for the first time, the road from Highway 12 into the park will be kept clear of snow.

Trail Information There are many trails in the park, especially to the east of the Bryce Canyon Lodge, and between Bryce Point and Fairyland Point, but these are day hikes only, with no camping permitted in that region. For the real hiker or person who wants to leave the tourists behind, there's the Under-The-Rim Trail. This trail runs from Bryce Point in the north to Rainbow Point in the extreme south. There are a series of connecting trails which can be used to make the trip shorter for those not wanting to walk the entire 35 kms. These connecting trails are named: Sheep Creek, Swamp Canyon, Whiteman, and Agua Canyon Trails. There's also an extension of this Under-The-Rim Trail running from Yovimpa Point to Rainbow Point, making the trail length 45 kms. There are several springs around Rainbow Point, but nowhere else — so you'll have to carry all your water.

Best Time and Time Needed This is a relatively high trail, so it can be walked in the mid-summer heat, from about late May through October. Depending on what time of day you begin the hike, this 35 km hike can be done in two or three days. But carrying water all that way makes for a heavy pack. Perhaps a connecting trail could be used to return to the rim so as to procure water from passing tourists? Consult park rangers at the visitor center before attempting this hike, for the latest information on usable springs in the canyon.

Campgrounds There are two campgrounds in Bryce Canyon, but they're always crowded. Camp elsewhere if peace, quiet and cheap camping is desired.

Maps Utah Travel Council Map 5 — Southwestern Utah, U.S.G.S. maps Panguitch, Kanab (1:100,000), Bryce Canyon National Park (1:31,680)

Typical Bryce Canyon scene. Pink rocks, blue sky and green trees (105mm lens).

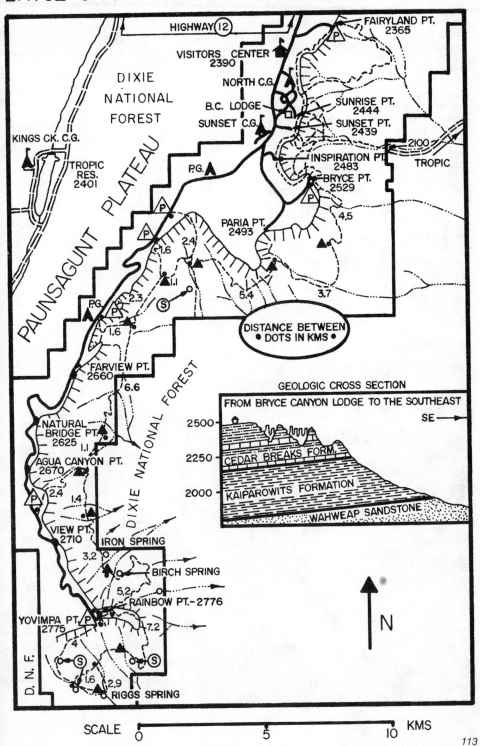

HIGHWAY (12)

VISITORS CENTER
2390

NORTH C.G.

B.C. LODGE

SUNSET C.G.

DIXIE
NATIONAL
FOREST

KINGS CK. C.G.

TROPIC
RES.
2401

PAUNSAGUNT PLATEAU

P.G.

FAIRYLAND PT.
2365

SUNRISE PT.
2444

SUNSET PT.
2439

2100

TROPIC

INSPIRATION PT.
2483

BRYCE PT.
2529

PARIA PT.
2493

4.5

2.4

1.6

1.1

2.3

1.6

5.4

3.7

DISTANCE BETWEEN
• DOTS IN KMS •

FARVIEW PT.
2660

6.6

DIXIE NATIONAL FOREST

NATURAL
BRIDGE PT.
2625

1.1

AGUA CANYON PT.
2670

2.4

1.4

GEOLOGIC CROSS SECTION

FROM BRYCE CANYON LODGE TO THE SOUTHEAST

SE →

2500

CEDAR BREAKS FORM.

2250

KAIPAROWITS FORMATION

2000

WAHWEAP SANDSTONE

VIEW PT.
2710

IRON SPRING

3.2

BIRCH SPRING

5.2

RAINBOW PT.- 2776

YOVIMPA PT.
2775

7.2

N

4

D.N.F.

1.6

2.9

RIGGS SPRING

SCALE

0   5   10

KMS

48. Upper Escalante River

Location This map covers the upper end of the Escalante River, located in extreme south-central Utah, not far north of the Arizona state line, and just east of Escalante.

Geology Highest mesas and plateaus in the area are capped by Carmel Formation. Under that is Navajo Sandstone. This is exposed in the canyon walls between Escalante and Horse Canyon. In the lower Escalante R. the Kayenta and Wingate Sandstones are exposed and form the steep and narrow canyons in that region.

Fremont Ruins Found in most canyons of the Upper Escalante River are ruins from the Fremont Indian Culture. They're from the same time as Anasazis, but lived and farmed in the canyon bottoms. Storage granaries are seen on cliffs.

Access Utah Highway 12, running between Panguitch, Escalante and on to Torrey is the only road to this area. From Highway 12, the Pine Creek Road runs north of Escalante; the Burr Trail runs east of Boulder; and the Hole-In-the-Rock Road runs southeast from Escalante.

Trail Information Not many trails here, almost all hiking is done in the canyon bottoms or in the stream itself. Because of the high altitude of the drainage, all the major canyons have year-round flowing streams. The walk through Death Hollow begins north of Escalante, and 3 or 4 kms east of Pine Creek Campground. The upper part is dry, but lower down it has a nice stream. At one point about 3 kms north of the Escalante River, is a large, deep hole. Swimming is required to cross it, with an air mattress or inner tube to float packs across. Most water in the Escalante R. is ankle to knee deep. Another hike is from Escalante to Highway 12. Some park at Highway 12-Escalante River, and come out the Harris Wash. The Gulch, Horse Canyon and Deer Creek are other entry points. Calf Creek is a popular day hike, with ruins and pictographs. At the bottom of the map is 25 Mile Wash and the Egypt entry points, one of the most popular in the whole Escalante River. The road going to Pine Creek C.G. and the Hole-in-the-Rock Road are very good. All raods on the map are open to all cars most of the time. Do not hike without consulting the BLM office in Escalante for up-to-date conditions. Best footwear is canvas boots, but running shoes are often used.

Best Time and Time Needed The Death Hollow hike should be done from late June to mid-September, but hike other areas from late May on through October. With cold water, spring and fall are not the best times to hike here. The Death Hollow Hike to Escalante is about 3 days. From Highway 12 to Escalante R. and up Harris, about 3 days with car shuttle.

Campgrounds Many excellent campsites along creek bottoms. All streams have good water, but the Escalante River water, below Escalante town, should be boiled or treated.

Maps Utah Travel Council Maps 1 and 5, Southwestern and Southeastern Utah, BLM map "Hiking the Escalante River", U.S.G.S. maps Escalante (1:100,000)

This is typical scenery from the upper part of the Escalante River (105mm lens).

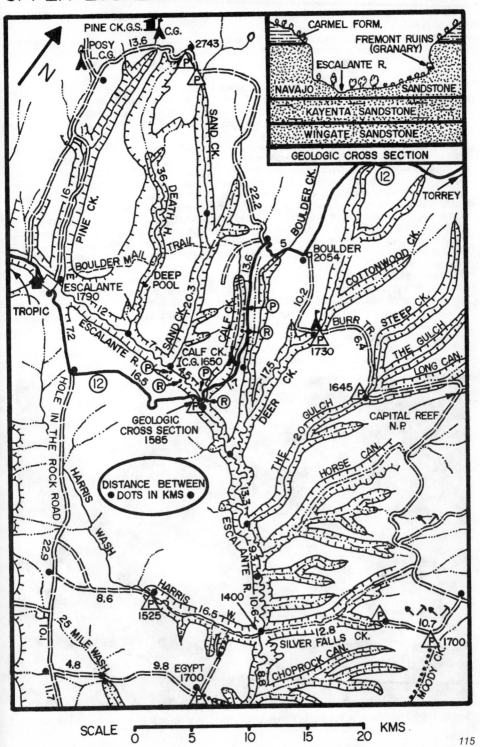

PINE CK. G.S.   C.G.
POSY L. C.G.   13.6
2743

SAND CK.

GEOLOGIC CROSS SECTION

CARMEL FORM.
FREMONT RUINS
(GRANARY)
ESCALANTE R.
NAVAJO   SANDSTONE
KAYENTA SANDSTONE
WINGATE SANDSTONE
GEOLOGIC CROSS SECTION

TORREY
BOULDER CK.
12
5
BOULDER
2054
COTTONWOOD CK.

16.1
PINE CK.
.36
DEATH H. TRAIL
BOULDER MAIL TRAIL
22.2
13.6
10.2
STEEP CK.
BURR TR.
THE GULCH
6.4
LONG CAN.

ESCALANTE
1790
DEEP POOL
SAND CK. 20.3
CALF CK.

TROPIC
7.2
ESCALANTE R.   7
12
16.5
CALF CK.
I.C.G. 1650
4.5
17.5
DEER CK.
1730
1645
CAPITAL REEF N.P.
THE .20 GULCH
HORSE CAN.

12
GEOLOGIC CROSS SECTION
1585

DISTANCE BETWEEN
● DOTS IN KMS ●

HOLE IN THE ROCK ROAD
HARRIS WASH
22.9
13.3
9.3
ESCALANTE R.

8.6
HARRIS
1525
16.5 W.
1400
10.6
10.7
1700
MOODY CK.

10.1
25 MILE WASH
4.8
11.7
9.8 EGYPT
1700
12.8
SILVER FALLS CK.
CHOPROCK CAN.
8.8

SCALE   0   5   10   15   20   KMS

49. Lower Escalante River

Location This map covers the lower or bottom end of the Escalante River, located in extreme southern Utah, very near the Arizona state line. It's between Bryce Canyon and Capital Reef N.P. and Glen Canyon N.R.A.

Geology Most of the canyon walls here are made up of the Navajo Sandstone, as is the case in the Coyote Gulch. The geologic cross section shows one arch and one of several huge undercuts. Further to the east and downstream, one can observe the Kayenta and Wingate Sandstones and Chinle Formation.

Access: All parts of the lower Escalante River can be reached via the Hole-in-the-Rock Road. This road begins about 8 kms southeast of the town of Escalante and ends at the Hole-in-the-Rock Historical Marker. This is where the Mormon San Juan Mission Party cut a trail down through the cliff and eventually took wagons and livestock across the Colorado River. The last 5 kms of road is good, but next-to-last 5 kms is rough. Any car can make it — with care. One can also use the Burr Trail to reach Moody Creek. Always drive more cautiously when on side roads leading off the Hole-in-the-Rock Road.

Trail Information Few trails here, just walk in the canyon bottoms. Water is always present in lower canyons, most of which can be used without treatment. But treat Escalante River water. Best footwear is high-topped canvas boots, but most use running shoes. You'll be in water perhaps 1/10 of the time, depending on the canyon. Water is ankle to knee deep. The most popular canyon for hikers is Coyote Gulch. Walk into this canyon where Hurricane Gulch crosses the road, or one could also walk in or out from 40 Mile Ridge or Red Well. Another popular hike is to park at Egypt, walk down the Escalante, then up 25 Mile Gulch and back to the car. Choprock, the Moodys and Stevens Canyons are interesting. There are many other entry points, most of which are shown on the map. Before hiking, always stop at the BLM and Glen Canyon N.R.A. office west of Escalante, for free maps and up-date information on roads and water.

Best Time and Time Needed Best time to visit the lower Escalante River is in spring and fall. May, June, September and October are best times. Mid-summer is warm, but there's always a river to jump into. The author parked at the Hurricane Gulch Trailhead (on the Hole-in-the-Rock Road) walked down to the first arch, shot a roll of film, and returned in 5½ hours. Many do this hike to the Escalante River and maybe a side canyon or two, in two days, maybe three.

Campgrounds Camp anywhere, but take climber's stove. Possibly mosquitos in summer.

Maps Utah Travel Council Map 1 — Southeastern Utah, BLM map "Hiking the Escalante River", U.S.G.S. maps Smokey Mtn., Escalante (1:100,000)

This is Jacob Hamblin Arch in Coyote Gulch, Lower Escalante River (17mm lens).

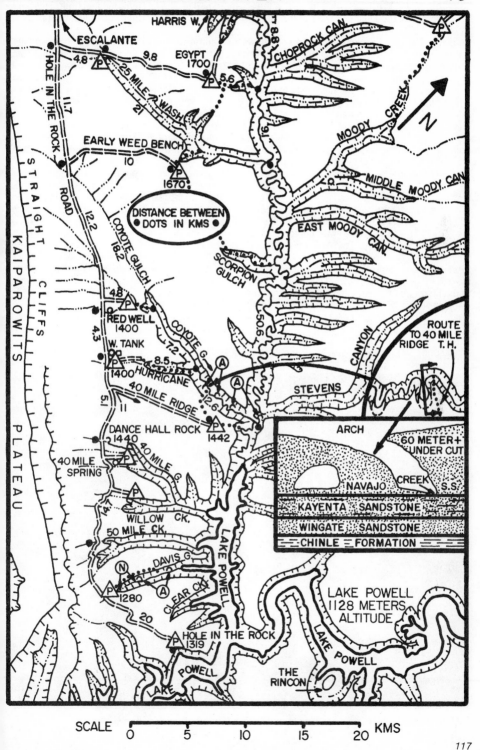

SCALE   0   5   10   15   20   KMS

50. Muley Twist Canyon, Capital Reef National Park

Location Muley Twist Canyon is located in the southern part of Capital Reef National Park. This park lies in south-central Utah just west of the Henry Mountains, with its northern parts just east of Loa, Bicknell and Torrey.

Geology The small geologic cross section shows the central parts of the Waterpocket Fold, and the highest portion called the Capital Reef. This cross section is of the lower end of the canyon and cuts through a large overhang or undercut of perhaps 55-60 meters. Graffiti here dates from the 1920's and was apparently a cowboy camp. In this area the massive vertical cliffs are mostly made from the Navajo Sandstone. One of the most interesting features of Muley Twist Canyon is three large undercuts, all ranging from 50 to 60 meters in depth.

Access Most people coming here first call at the national park visitor center located further north at Fruita. They then drive east 20 kms on Utah Highway 24 to where the Notom-Bullfrog Road turns south. After about 56 kms is the junction of the Burr Trail and Notom-Bullfrog Roads. The Burr Trail begins in Boulder on Utah Highway 12 to the west. These are the only two roads reaching this region. Both roads are well maintained and can be used by any vehicle.

Trail Information Muley Twist Canyon has no trail, just walk in the dry creek bed. The standard hike for most people is to park at the Burr Trail Trailhead, walk down the canyon to Halls Creek (always dry), then north to The Post. If it's a large party, one car is left there so the last 6.8 kms of road walking can be eliminated. Most take it in two days. The author made a very fast one day hike out of this route, walking a full circle in about 7½ hours. If you've got one day only, it's recommended you park at The Post and use the Cut-Off Trail to reach the lower portion of Muley Twist, which is the best part anyway. Most could do this hike in one long day. There's no *reliable* source of water in the canyon. Carry water in your car and on your back. The hike is over sand and gravel, so any hiking boot or running shoe is good.

Best Time and Time Needed Many hike down from the Burr Trail, and return the same day. Others make a more leisurely hike in two days. Best time to hike is spring and fall, namely April, May, June, September and October. July and August are too hot.

Campgrounds Park rules state; no camping outside designated campsites, except when backcountry hiking. If you're at the Butt Trail Trailhead late in the P.M., one merely needs to walk to a point out of sight of the road and drop a tent.

Maps Utah Travel Council Map 1 — Southeastern Utah, and U.S.G.S. maps Escalante, Hite Crossing (1:100,000), Wagon Box Mesa, Mt. Pennel (1:62,500)

Huge undercut, called Cowboy Camp by author. It's 50-60 meters deep (17mm lens).

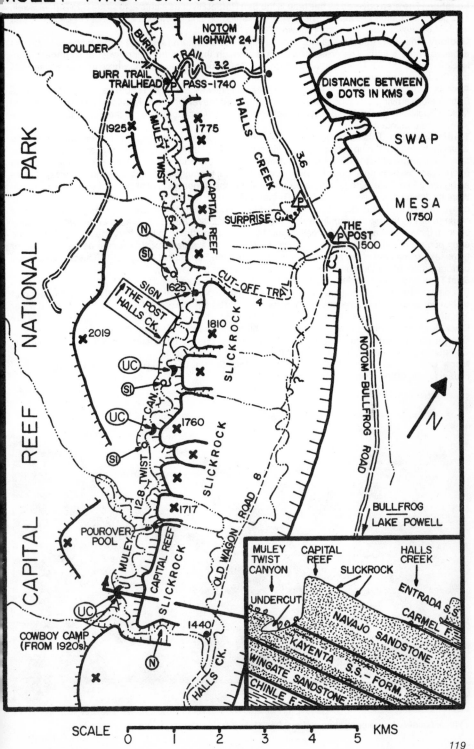

51. San Rafael River, San Rafael Swell

Location The area covered by this map is the San Rafael River as it cuts across the San Rafael Swell. The general location is south of Price, east of Huntington and Castle Dale, west of Green River, and north of the newly built Interstate Highway 70.

Geology The San Rafael Swell is a large, uplifted dome feature (anticline) and has the oldest rocks exposed in the center. The cross section cuts through the swell from northwest to southeast, from Buckhorn Well to I-70. There's a slight nonconformity around the Black Box, where the San Rafael cuts into Coconino Sandstone.

Access Most people reach the heart of the area via Highway 29 running southwest out of Price. About 3 kms before arriving at Castle Dale, turn east on a good gravel road, which passes the pumphouse and tank at Buckhorn Well. Then descend Buckhorn Wash (with pictographs) to the San Rafael C.G. The same road continues to I-70.

Trail Information This hasn't been a backpackers area, so there are no trails. The two most interesting areas for hiking are the upper and lower ends of the San Rafael River. One hike is this: drive southwest from Buckhorn Well to the river, then walk downstream to the San Rafael C.G. River crossings are knee deep. Wear old running shoes or canvas boots. There are tamarisks, sagebrush and cottonwood trees along the 25 km hike. The second area of interest is the upper and lower parts of the Black Box. Get there by driving southeast from the San Rafael C.G. to near the end of the road. One can then enter the canyon above the Upper Black Box and wade down through to near Mexican Mountain. At that point one could return to the car, or continue down to the Lower Black Box and Swazys Leap (with old sheep bridge). If overnighting with large pack, better take an air mattress to help ferry the pack across some deep pools. For short hikes, take your own water, and always have lots in your car as well. For longer hikes take some kind of tablets to purify water, or boil the San Rafael River water. There's some good petroglyphs in Black Dragon Canyon (near the east side of the map).

Best Time and Time Needed Best time for hiking here is in spring and fall. But if you're doing the Black Box hike where you'll be in deep water, the fall is best, September and October. If hiking the upper part of the river down to the campground, then spring would be equally good. There'll be high and cold water 'till June 1 each year. You'll need two days for the upper river hike, with car shuttle, and 4 days for the Black Box hike. Shorter, in-and-out same-day hikes can also be made in all areas.

Campgrounds San Rafael Campground is a primitive one with no water, but with fine shade trees. Campsites everywhere along the river. Mosquitos in summer too.

Maps Utah Travel Council Map 2 — Southeastern Central Utah, U.S.G.S. maps Huntington, San Rafael (1:100,000). There are many maps at 1:24,000 scale.

Typical scenery in the central part of the San Rafael River, San Rafael Swell (35mm lens).

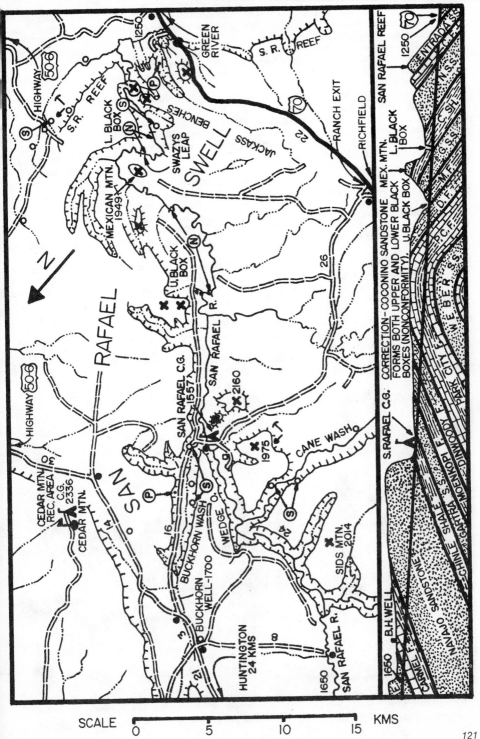

SCALE

0   5   10   15   KMS

52. The Needles, Canyonlands National Park

Location Canyonlands National Park lies in southeastern Utah, just to the southwest of Moab, and between Arches National Park and Lake Powell. It covers the area where the Green and Colorado Rivers meet, a place often called The Confluence. There are three separate parts to Canyonlands; The Island in the Sky, The Maze and The Needles.

Geology The geologic cross section is an exaggerated look at the land running from about Elephant Canyon to the Colorado. All features seen between Peekaboo Spring, Druid Arch, and Squaw Flat C.G. are part of the Cedar Mesa Sandstone. To the west are small graben valleys, apparently caused by the dissolving of Paradox Salt.

Access Access to this part of Canyonlands is made very easy by the recent paving of State Road 211, which runs from the highway connecting Moab with Monticello, to The Needles. It's paved to as far as Squaw Flat Campground. There's a good gravel road running from the campground to Elephant Hill Trailhead, but all other roads in The Needles are for 4WD's only. The distance from Highway 163 to the campgrounds is about 63 kms, and passes a wall 0f pictographs known as Newspaper Rock.

Trail Information All three parts of Canyonlands are very interesting and beautiful, but The Needles is much more developed, especially the hiking trails. Therefore expect to see more people in this part and on the trails. The trails here are well marked, with good sign posts indicating routes and distances. When trails cross slickrock (barren, smooth rock), small stone carins mark the way. The two trailheads where everyone starts, are at the campground and Elephant Hill. Most people using these trails end up at Druid Arch or Chesler Park. Another popular hike after parking at Elephant Hill, is to walk down Red Lake Canyon to the Colorado River. Check current road conditions at the visitor center to see if your vehicle can go beyond the Hill. Always carry water for your entire trip, as the few springs there are intermittent.

Best Time and Time Needed The best time to hike here is in spring or fall. Late April, May, June, September, and October are the very best times to visit The Needles. July and August are simply too hot to enjoy, usually. For this area short day hikes are most common. Druid Arch and Chesler Park are all-day hikes. If you have a 4WD, then the hike to the Colorado River is a one day hike, otherwise it's two or three days.

Campgrounds There's a fine campground at Squaw Flat, complete with a large semi-truck trailer with water tank. Stock up here before doing any hike. The campground is for a fee and is full most of the time. Camp elsewhere if you don't like crowds.

Maps Utah Travel Council Map 1 — Southeastern Utah, U.S.G.S. maps La Sal (1:100,000), Canyonlands National Park (1:62,500), The Needles (1:62,500)

Druid Arch, located in the southern part of The Needles (35mm lens).

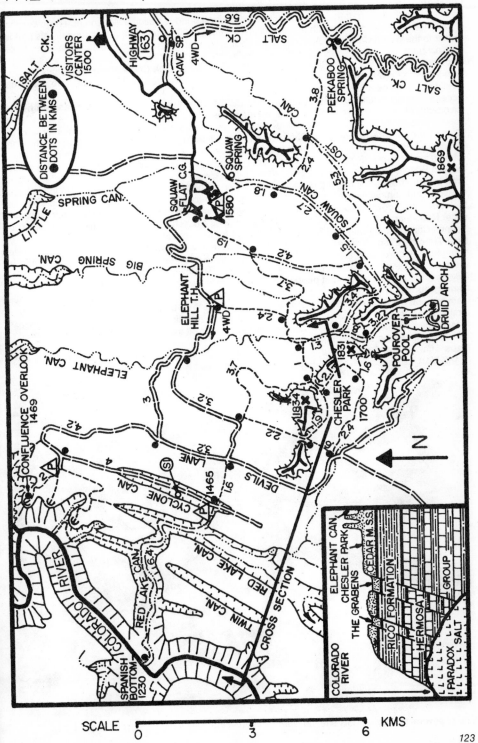

53. Dark Canyon

Location Dark Canyon is located directly west of the Abajo Mountains, and east of Hite Marina on Lake Powell, in southeastern Utah. It's also due north of Natural Bridges National Monument. The lower end of Dark Canyon is very deep with steep walls rising about 500 meters to the mesa tops. This part is similar to the Grand Canyon of Arizona with a clear stream at the bottom. Some upper canyons have Anasazi ruins.

Geology Near the Colorado River, now Lake Powell, one sees the Cedar Mesa Sandstone on top, then the Rico Formation, and below the mouth of Black Steer Canyon the Hermosa Group, made up mostly of limestone and shale.

Access Since the building of Glen Canyon Dam and the creation of Lake Powell, some people arrive at the mouth of Dark Canyon by boat. Most however, prefer to hike into Dark Canyon Primitive Area. Most popular entry point is at the head of Woodenshoe Canyon. Reach this place by driving along Highway 95, then turn off to the Bridges N.M. One km from the junction, turn off on a dirt road and proceed through the Bears Ears to a parking place near the corral, as shown. One can reach the bottom end of Dark Canyon via Highway 95, not far from Hite. Turn northeast onto a dirt road just to the west of the White Canyon Bridge, and follow signs to Sundance Trail.

Trail Information Most walking is done in the dry creek bed or along side the stream in lower Dark Canyon. Other entry points are Black Steer, Youngs, Lean-to, and Trail Canyons. Many people park at the corral, walk down Woodenshoe, into Dark Canyon to the lower end, then retrace their steps 'till upper Dark, then exit at Peavine Canyon. This eliminates a car shuttle. The author did this trip down to Youngs Canyon and return in 3 full days. It's 5 days for most people.

Best Time and Time Needed If the average hiker were to walk down Woodenshoe, to Lake Powell, then return and exit at Peavine, it would take very close to one week. A good and short hike for those with little time, would be to walk down the Sundance Trail. The lower part of Dark is the best part anyway. July and August heat turns most people off, so most hiking is done in Spring and Fall.

Campgrounds There are many campsites in the canyon, but not much water above Black Steer Canyon. The intermittent running water shown was what the author encountered after heavy September rains of 1982. Don't enter the upper parts of the canyon until consulting the rangers at Bridges N.M. or the Kane Gulch Ranger Station concerning the current availability of water. Running shoes or canvas "jungle" boots are recommended.

Maps Utah Travel Council Map 1 — Southeastern Utah, U.S.G.S. maps Hite Crossing, Blanding (1:100,000), Lower Dark Canyon, Fable Valley, Bear Ears (1:62,500)

One of several pourover pools seen in Dark Canyon. Middle sections of canyon (35mm lens).

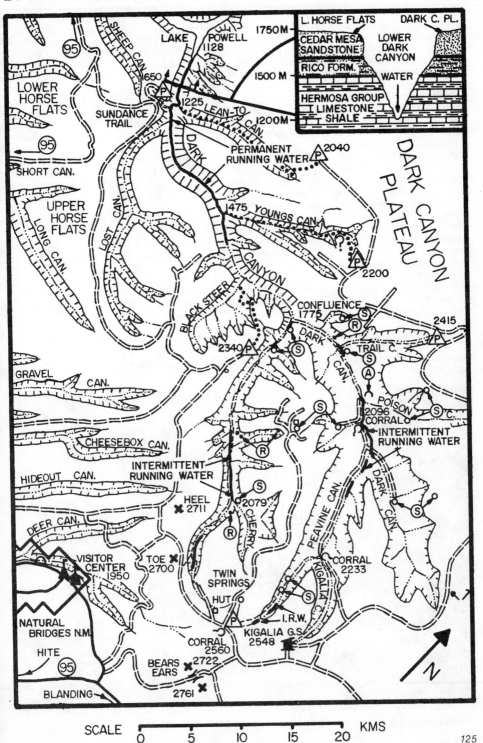

SCALE

0   5   10   15   20   KMS

54. Natural Bridges National Monument

Location Featured here is the Natural Bridges National Monument and a canyon hike which takes hikers down one canyon and up another, passing enroute three of the world's largest natural bridges, and Anasazi ruins. Bridges is located about half-way between Blanding and Hite Marina on Lake Powell, and just southwest of the Abajo Mountains.

Geology The geologic cross section on the map shows a section cutting through the Sipapu Bridge, but also includes other formations extending beyond the park boundaries. At the viewpoint overlooking Sipapu Bridge, visitors stand on Cedar Mesa Sandstone. The other diagram shows in simplified form, the making of a bridge.

Access Access is from Highway 95 running from Blanding to Hite Marina. Take the Bridges road northwest from 95 to the visitor center, where additional maps and information can be found. Also visit the Photovoltaic Array, or solar power plant nearby. This facility produces all electric power for the park. From the visitor center the road runs west to the Bridge View Drive Circle, a 13 km loop with many parking places.

Trail Information At the three viewpoints overlooking each bridge is a parking place and a trail leading down into the canyon. These are maintained trails and well used. But the emphasis here is the canyon hike from the Sipapu Bridge, down White Canyon to Kachina Bridge, then up stream in Armstrong Canyon to Owachomo Bridge. The parts of this hike between bridges are unmaintained trails. Most walking is done in the dry creek bed. Any kind of hiking boot or even running shoes will do. There's no reliable source of water in the canyons, so take all water needed for the hike. There's a maintained and marked trail crossing the mesa connecting all three points of entry into the canyons. Very near the confluence of Deer and White Canyons are some pictographs under an overhang. Three hundred meters further down the canyon and on the west side, are Anasazi ruins.

Best Time and Time Needed Best time to hike through these canyons is in spring and fall, thus avoiding the heat of summer in July and August. May, June, September and October are the most pleasant months for walking here. April and November are generally too cold, but in some years they can be mild. If you're starting and parking at Sipapu, and will hike in the canyons all the way to Owachomo, then on the mesa trail back to Sipapu, plan for an all day outing. This walking loop is about 12 or 13 kms.

Campgrounds The only place one can camp inside the park boundaries is at Bridges Campgrounds not far from the visitor center. No camping permitted in the canyons.

Maps Utah Travel Council Map 1 — Southeastern Utah, U.S.G.S. maps Hite Crossing, Blanding (1:100,000), Natural Bridges (1:62,500)

Huge pourover pool near Kachina Bridge. It's usually full of water (17mm lens).

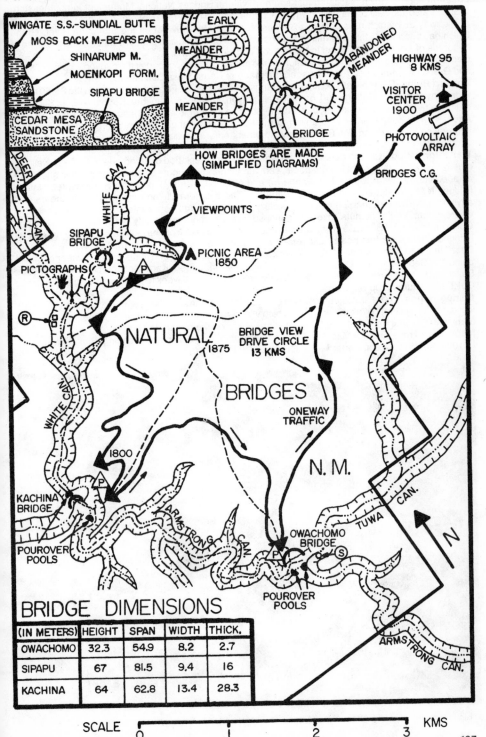

WINGATE S.S.–SUNDIAL BUTTE
MOSS BACK M.–BEARS EARS
SHINARUMP M.
MOENKOPI FORM.
SIPAPU BRIDGE
CEDAR MESA SANDSTONE

EARLY MEANDER
MEANDER
LATER MEANDER
ABANDONED MEANDER
BRIDGE

HOW BRIDGES ARE MADE
(SIMPLIFIED DIAGRAMS)

HIGHWAY 95
8 KMS
VISITOR CENTER
1900
PHOTOVOLTAIC ARRAY
BRIDGES C.G.

DEER CAN.
WHITE CAN.
VIEWPOINTS
SIPAPU BRIDGE
PICTOGRAPHS
PICNIC AREA
1850
P
NATURAL 1875
BRIDGE VIEW DRIVE CIRCLE
13 KMS
BRIDGES
ONEWAY TRAFFIC
N.M.
WHITE CAN.
1800
P
KACHINA BRIDGE
POUROVER POOLS
ARMSTRONG CAN.
OWACHOMO BRIDGE
P
S
TUWA CAN.
POUROVER POOLS
ARMSTRONG CAN.
N

BRIDGE DIMENSIONS

(IN METERS)	HEIGHT	SPAN	WIDTH	THICK.
OWACHOMO	32.3	54.9	8.2	2.7
SIPAPU	67	81.5	9.4	16
KACHINA	64	62.8	13.4	28.3

SCALE   0   1   2   3   KMS

55. Grand Gulch

Location Grand Gulch is located just south of Natural Bridges National Monument in southeastern Utah. It's also just east of State Highway 263, formerly the old Mormon Hole-in-the-Rock Trail, and west of Highway 261 which runs between Bridges N.M. and Mexican Hat on the San Juan River. Grand Gulch has been made into a primitive area because of its scenic and primitive nature, and because of hundreds of Anasazi ruins found in the canyon and side canyons.

Geology The little geologic cross section on the map is of the upper part of the canyon where the Kane and Grand Gulches meet. All rocks seen are made of Cedar Mesa Sandstone.

Anasazi Ruins Ruins always occupy overhangs and face south. Farming was done in the 25-50 meter wide canyon bottom. Cottonwood, gamble oak, pinyon, juniper and sagebrush in bottoms. In Slickhorn drainage farming was on mesa top. It's the best place in Utah to see and inspect Anasazi ruins.

Access Most people enter the canyon at the Kane Gulch Ranger Station after getting last minute information, then exit through Bullet Canyon. Others enter or exit at Collins Spring, while extra hardy people may enter in the upper canyon somewhere and exit via the Slickhorn Canyon.

Trail Information No real trails here, just walk in the dry creek bed or along one side. Easy walking, mostly in sand. Light-weight leather boots, canvas "jungle" type boots and common running shoes are all adequate footwear. Contact the ranger(s) at the Kane Gulch R.S. or at the visitor center, Natural Bridges N.M., for updates on the water situation. There is normally no running water in the canyon anywhere, only occasional springs. Always carry some water, and if encountering other hikers ask of its whereabouts. You'll "go nuts" over the ruins, so take a camera and plenty of film. If parking at Kane Gulch and exiting at Bullet Canyon, one can usually get a ride back on the highway. Places where water is found in this and other nearby canyons are referred to as "seeps," rather than springs.

Best Time and Time Needed Most hikers do this trip in April, May and June, with a number of others doing it in September and October. July and August are hot. From Kane Gulch R.S. down Grand, up Bullet and back to the Kane Gulch R.S. is 2 long or 3 easy days. A week to 10 days if doing entire Grand Gulch and returning up Slickhorn.

Campgrounds There are countless good campsites in the canyon. It's recommended at least one 3½ liter jug (1 US gallon) be taken, for water, which will allow hikers to camp in areas not near seeps. Also, carry water in your vehicle, there's no water anywhere on the rim or plateau.

Maps Utah Travel Council Map 1 — Southeastern Utah, U.S.G.S. maps Blanding, Bluff, Navajo Mtn. (1:100,000), Bears Ears, Cedar Mesa, Grand Gulch (1:62:500)

This is but one of many Anasazi ruins seen in Grand Gulch (17mm lens).

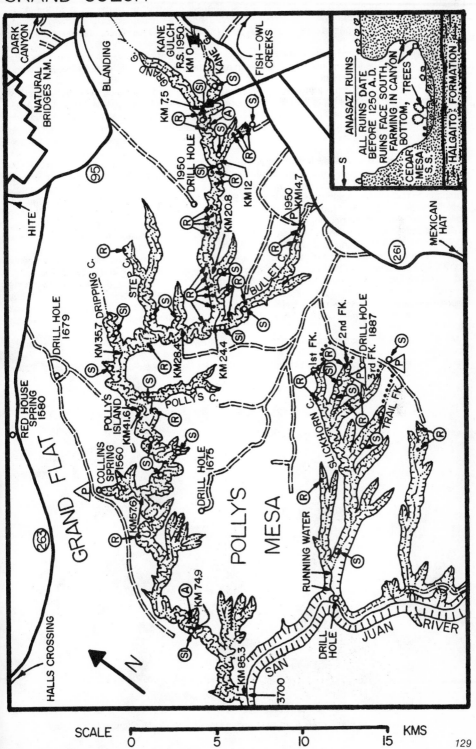

SCALE

0   5   10   15 KMS

56. Fish and Owl Creeks

Location This mapped area is located in the southeastern corner of Utah, south of the Abajo Mountains and north of the San Juan River. It's also sandwiched inbetween US Highway 163 and Highway 261. Fish Creek has several places with permanent running water. There are even small fish in one section.

Geology As the geologic cross section shows these streams have cut deep canyons into the Cedar Mesa Sandstone. The flat-topped plateau is known as Cedar Mesa and is about 1850 meters altitude. Canyons are 200-250 meters deep.

Anasazi Ruins This is both a primitive area and has ruins; second best place in Utah to see ruins. Ruins face south to catch the winter sun. Farming here was on mesa tops. Inhabitants left by 1250 A.D.

Access Drive south from Utah Highway 95 (running between Blanding and Lake Powell) on Highway 261 from the area around Natural Bridges N.M. to a point about 3 kms south of the Kane Gulch Ranger Station. Then turn east and drive about 8 kms on a good dirt road to where the road ends at a drill hole and trail head.

Trail Information There are few trails in these canyons, but there's little need for them. Simply follow the dry stream beds or walk along the small streams. Most people hiking in this drainage walk down Fish and up Owl Creek. From the drill hole, where is located a trail register, walk north-northeast using a compass, to the rim overlooking the confluence of Fish Creek's two upper tributaries. Once at the rim, search for one of two or three routes down into the canyon. Once in the canyon the way is easy. Coming up from Owl Creek is a trail beginning at about point 1585 meters. There are stone carins along the way to the drill hole. Best hiking boots here are light-weight leather hiking boots, but jungle boots are also popular as are common running shoes.

Best Time and Time Needed July and August are too hot, making spring and fall ideal. Most people make the hike in spring — April, May or June, with others coming in September and October. The author did this hike in one long and tiresome day, but most people spend one night and sometimes two in the canyon. Round trip distance is about 25 kms. Running water as of October 1982, just after heavy September rains, are as shown. Only bathers may pollute the water. It's good for drinking. Water isn't the problem here as in other canyons. Always consult the rangers at Kane Gulch Ranger Station before entering the canyons.

Campgrounds Camping can be done at the trailhead or anywhere in the canyons, as good sites are abundant everywhere. Have a supply of water in your car, as there's none on the mesa.

Maps Utah Travel Council Map 1 — Southeastern Utah, U.S.G.S. maps Bluff (1:100,000), Bluff, Cedar Mesa (1:62,000)

These Anasazi ruins are 500 meters from trailhead in Upper Fish Creek Canyon (35mm lens).

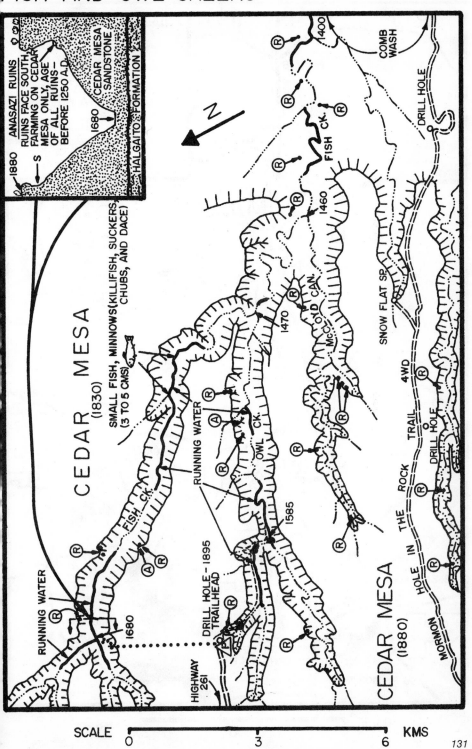

ANASAZI RUINS
RUINS FACE SOUTH
FARMING ON CEDAR
MESA ONLY, AGE
OF ALL RUINS
BEFORE 1250 A.D.

1880

S

1680

CEDAR MESA
SANDSTONE

HALGAITO FORMATION

N

1400

COMB WASH

DRILL HOLE

FISH CK.

1460

SNOW FLAT SP.

CEDAR MESA
(1830)

SMALL FISH, MINNOWS(KILLIFISH, SUCKERS, CHUBS, AND DACE)
(3 TO 5 CMS)

McCLOYD CAN.

1470

RUNNING WATER

OWL CK.

4WD

DRILL HOLE

1585

HOLE IN THE ROCK TRAIL

RUNNING WATER

FISH CK.

1680

DRILL HOLE – 1895
TRAILHEAD

CEDAR MESA
(1880)

HIGHWAY 261

MORMON

NATIONAL FORESTS AND PARKS OF UTAH

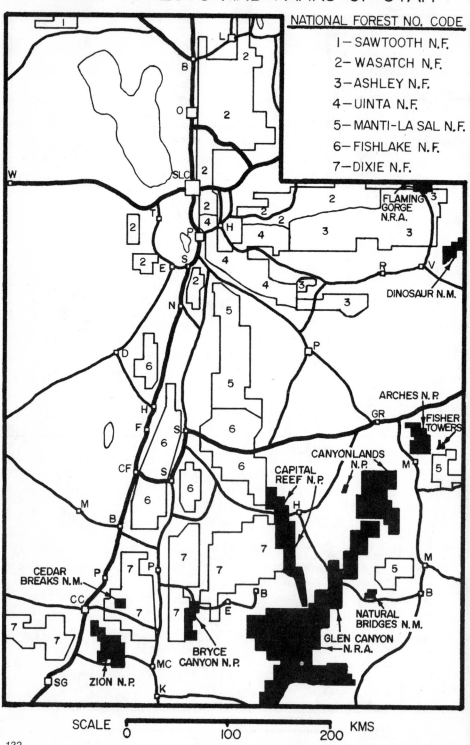

NATIONAL FOREST NO. CODE

1 – SAWTOOTH N.F.
2 – WASATCH N.F.
3 – ASHLEY N.F.
4 – UINTA N.F.
5 – MANTI-LA SAL N.F.
6 – FISHLAKE N.F.
7 – DIXIE N.F.

FLAMING GORGE N.R.A.

DINOSAUR N.M.

ARCHES N.P.

FISHER TOWERS

CANYONLANDS N.P.

CAPITAL REEF N.P.

NATURAL BRIDGES N.M.

GLEN CANYON N.R.A.

CEDAR BREAKS N.M.

BRYCE CANYON N.P.

ZION N.P.

SCALE
0   100   200   KMS

List of Utahs 4000 meter Peaks (all in the Uinta Mts.)

List of Peaks over 3600 meters outside the Uinta Mountains

From the Loop Campground in Stansbury Mts. It's 7 kms to the top of Deseret Peak (35mm lens).

Heliograph Stations in Utah

Heliograph is the name of an instrument having a mirror set upon a tripod, which is used to send signals by using the rays of the sun. These contraptions were used in the early years of geodetic surveys in the western USA. Some of these first surveys in Utah were made from about 1882 on through the late 1880's.

The Heliographs were set upon high and prominent peaks, then triangulation measurements were taken to determine altitudes and locations. On some major summits, surveyers were camped for extended periods of time. On those summits stone sleeping huts and flat triangulation platforms were constructed. Some of these old structures are still standing and therein lies the reason for adding the subject to this book.

The map shows the Utah stations. This information comes from the U.S. Coast and Geodetic Survey of 1883 and uses names of peaks used at that time. Some names have changed: North Ogden is now likely to be Ben Lomond Peak; Vernon is probably Black Crook Peak in the Sheeprock Mountains; Gosiute is Ibapah Peak; Oak Creek is Fool Peak in the Canyon Range; Wasatch is Heliotrope Mtn. east of Gunnison; and La Sal must be Mt. Peale in the La Sal Mountains. Jeff Davis Peak just inside Nevada, is now called Wheeler Peak.

The author has been on top of all these summits except Pilot, Pioche and Cliff (in the eastern Book Cliffs somewhere), and has found some kind of ruins at or near the top of each. The very best ruins are found on the top of Belknap and Ibapah (Gosiute). At the very summit of each peak can be found several small stone huts. All that remain of course are the stone walls. They originally had either tents on top to form the roofs, or some kind of wooded roofs. There are scattered wood pieces at each site, some of which must have been used as platform or tripod material.

Other peaks which have some limited amounts of ruins are: Nebo, just south of the south summit, and Fool Peak (Oak Creek) just west of the summit and down a bit. Both of these are simple tent platforms, but some artifacts such as nails and broken bottles still can be found. On other peaks, camping places were simply not observed or were less noticeable.

About the only reading material the author has found about these Heliograph Sations has been in the old US Coast and Geodetic Survey reports dating from the early 1880's. These documents are found in only a few of the larger libraries of the state.

September snows bury ruins of the Heliograph Station on top of Belknap (35mm lens).

HELIOGRAPH STATIONS OF UTAH

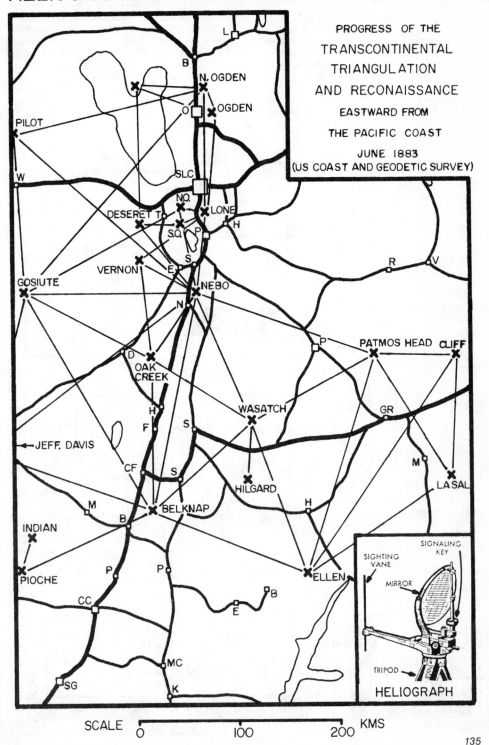

PROGRESS OF THE
TRANSCONTINENTAL
TRIANGULATION
AND RECONAISSANCE
EASTWARD FROM
THE PACIFIC COAST
JUNE 1883
(US COAST AND GEODETIC SURVEY)

L

B

N. OGDEN

O   OGDEN

PILOT

W

SLC

N.O.

DESERET T.   LONE
S.Q.   P   H
S
VERNON   E
GOSIUTE   NEBO
N   R   V
P
D   PATMOS HEAD   CLIFF
OAK
CREEK   GR
H   WASATCH   M
F   S
JEFF. DAVIS   LA SAL
CF   S
M   HILGARD   H
INDIAN   B   BELKNAP
P   P   H
PIOCHE   ELLEN
CC   B
E

MC

SG   K

SIGNALING
KEY
SIGHTING
VANE
MIRROR

TRIPOD

HELIOGRAPH

SCALE

0   100   200   KMS

Climographs of Utah

There are great climatic changes from northern Utah to the south eastern corner. Elevation directly affects the temperature, as does a town's situation in a valley or basin. Rainfall amounts vary greatly from north to south. The northern and western parts of the state receive the greatest amount of precipitation in fall, winter and especially in spring. But the south eastern portion of Utah has its highest precip in late summer — early fall. Compare Logan with Monticello. The northern part of Utah gets most of its precip from storms coming into the state from the northwest, west, or from the southwest. Southeastern Utah has higher amounts of precip from summer time thunder storms. This moisture usually comes from the south, around Baja California or the Gulf of Mexico. The Wasatch Front in northern Utah is affected by the Great Salt Lake. Areas from Brigham City to Salt Lake City occasionally have "lake effect" or "lake enhanced" storms. Of all valley locations in Utah, the higher bench areas of Bountiful receive the highest amounts of precipitation.

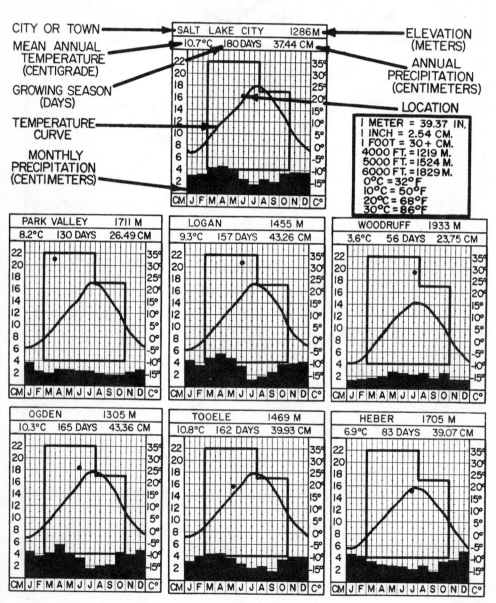

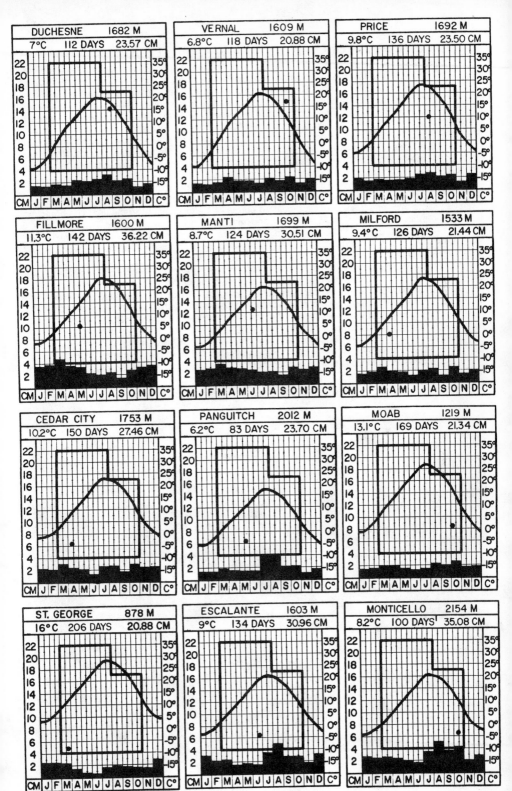

DUCHESNE 1682 M 7°C 112 DAYS 23.57 CM	**VERNAL** 1609 M 6.8°C 118 DAYS 20.88 CM	**PRICE** 1692 M 9.8°C 136 DAYS 23.50 CM
FILLMORE 1600 M 11.3°C 142 DAYS 36.22 CM	**MANTI** 1699 M 8.7°C 124 DAYS 30.51 CM	**MILFORD** 1533 M 9.4°C 126 DAYS 21.44 CM
CEDAR CITY 1753 M 10.2°C 150 DAYS 27.46 CM	**PANGUITCH** 2012 M 6.2°C 83 DAYS 23.70 CM	**MOAB** 1219 M 13.1°C 169 DAYS 21.34 CM
ST. GEORGE 878 M 16°C 206 DAYS 20.88 CM	**ESCALANTE** 1603 M 9°C 134 DAYS 30.96 CM	**MONTICELLO** 2154 M 8.2°C 100 DAYS 35.08 CM

Bristlecone Pines of Utah and the Western USA

If you're hiking or climbing in southwestern or western Utah, you should be aware of some of the trees in that region. The trees in question are the bristlecone pines, found only in the Great Basin of Utah, Arizona, Nevada and California. Depending on the book you read the official name is either *Pinus aristate* or *Pinus longaeva*. The name doesn't matter; the thing to remember is that it is likely the oldest living thing in the world. To the authors' knowledge, the oldest tree found is on Wheeler Peak in eastern Nevada. It's 4900 years old! In the White Mountains of California, east of Bishop, one is 4300 years old. The map shows the distribution according to several sources and the authors own climbs. The author has been to almost all these mountain areas, and questions the locations of some stands. He doubts bristlecone pines live on the Sevier Plateau (and in Colorado according to only one source), because of the higher amounts of moisture received, and other factors.

Typically, the bristlecone pine lives above 3000 meters, on poor rocky soil, and especially on soils derived from limestone. They grow 5 to 10 meters in height, are up to one meter in diameter, have needles in sets of 5, and have chocolate-colored cones with short bristles on the tips. The branches have needles clustered on the last 25 to 30 cms, and have the appearance of a fox tail. Trees are usually twisted, gnarled and squat and often half dead. Some have only a narrow piece of bark running up one side of the trunk which supports life. The most interesting trees are those on wind-swept ridges and other exposed locations, which often times grow horizontal instead of up.

In Utah, here are the known sites where bristlecone pines are found. The Deep Creek Range, on Swasy, Notch, Frisco and Indian Peaks, in the higher portions of the Wah Wah Mountains, and the northern part of the Mountain Home Range (just north of Indian Peak). They are likely to be in the Pine Valley Mountains, and on several scattered locations in Cedar Breaks National Monument and nearby plateaus. The stand most easily reached is the one on Spectra Point in Cedar Breaks, N.M. It's only about 1 km from the visitor center.

Outside of Utah they are found on Mt. Humphreys, Arizona, and in the White Mountains of California. They're also on most of the higher peaks of central and southern Nevada.

If you have seen bristlecone pine trees anywhere not listed on this map, please inform the author of their location.

From Spectra Point, Cedar Breaks N.M.; bristlecone pines, Cedar Breaks and Brian Head (35mm lens).

BRISTLECONE PINES OF UTAH, WESTERN USA

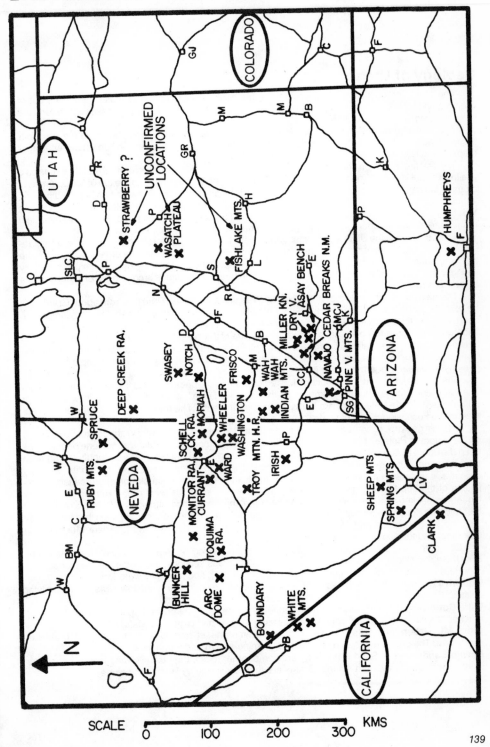

Geology of Utah

The short introduction to Utah geology in this book is not intended to make geologists out of climbers and hikers, bt merely to give the reader a simple introduction to the processes which form the mountains and plateaus of Utah.

The following map shows the locations of the geologic cross sections shown on the next four pages. In addition to the cross sections shown here, there are small cross sections on a number of other maps, especially the canyons on the Colorado Plateau.

The first cross section shows the Wellsville and Bear River Mountains in northern Utah. It runs on a line from about Honeyville just north of Brigham City, into the Cache Valley, to the top of Mt. Logan, and on east. Most of the formations in this area are limestone and dolomite. The area has been faulted and various blocks have been uplifted in relation to others. Therefore we have fault block mountains. Along with the faulting, great pressure has tilted some formations to about 45 degrees. These two mountain ranges are similar to other smaller mountains in the Great Basin of western Utah.

The next area is the Uinta Mountains. These mountains are a large oblong dome-shaped structure running east-west. The earth's crust buckled and forced the Uintas up, then later erosion wore down the higher regions. The result is the oldest rocks are exposed at the center of the range, with progressively younger rocks being exposed at the outer edges. The heart of the Uintas is composed of various layers of quartzite rock.

The next cross section is that of the central Wasatch Mountains. This runs from about Grandview Peak in the north, to Lone Peak in the south. Lots of limestone here, as well as shales, conglomerates, quartzites and finally granite. These formations have been bent in several places running north-south, and this whole range has been uplifted on the east side of the Wasatch Fault. This fault forms the zone between mountain and valley all along the Wasatch Front. Around Lone Peak and in Little Cottonwood Canyon, an intrusive body has also caused uplifting. This rock is usually known as temple granite but geology maps call it quartz monzonite.

The Wasatch Plateau is another uplifted region, with all the beds of rock still in a horizontal position. The top of the plateau, generally known as the "Skyline Drive", is very flat. Along either side, near Ephraim and Castle Dale, there are faults running north-south. The rocks here are sandstone, limestone and an occasional vein of shale.

The last geologic cross section is that of the Henry Mountains and nearby Waterpocket Fold. This is on the Colorado Plateau, famous for its very flat-lying sandstone beds. But the sandstone bedding has been disrupted by the intrusive body which forms the heart of the Henrys. This was moulten magma in the beginning, but later cooled before reaching the surface. Later erosion left the diorite porphyry exposed. It is seen in the highest summits of the Henry Mountains. Crustal pressure caused some folding of the upper crust, resulting in the Waterpocket Fold, to the west of the Henrys. The Henry Mountains are known as laccolith mountains or sometimes laccolithic intrusions. Within the confines of the Colorado Plateau are 8 such mountains or ranges falling into this category. Besides the Henrys they are: the La Sal, Abajo and Navajo Mountains in Utah; the Rico, Ute and La Plata Mountains in Colorado; and the Carrizo Mountains in Arizona.

One of the best single sources of information is the Geological Highway Map of Utah, put out by B.Y.U. Geology Dept. It has the geologic map of Utah, cross sections, and some brief explanations.

Here are several of the better known formations in Utah and how they were formed.

Oquirrh Formation (mostly limestone) — It was layed down in warm shallow seas, and was later uplifted. Composed mostly of marine shells, and corals (seen in central Wasatch Mts.).

Little Cottonwood Quartz Monzonite (granite) — Molten magma pushed up from below, but never reached the surface. It cooled very slowly, forming the salt and pepper crystals.

Uinta Mt. Group (quartzite) — It's usually metamorphosed (combining of heat and pressure) sandstone. The grains are then recrystallized, forming a hard and tough rock.

Navajo Sandstone — Sand is made by erosion of other rocks, then usually wind blown, often near shallow seas and in a desert setting. Grains are then cemented by lime or iron oxide.

LOCATIONS OF GEOLOGIC CROSS SECTIONS

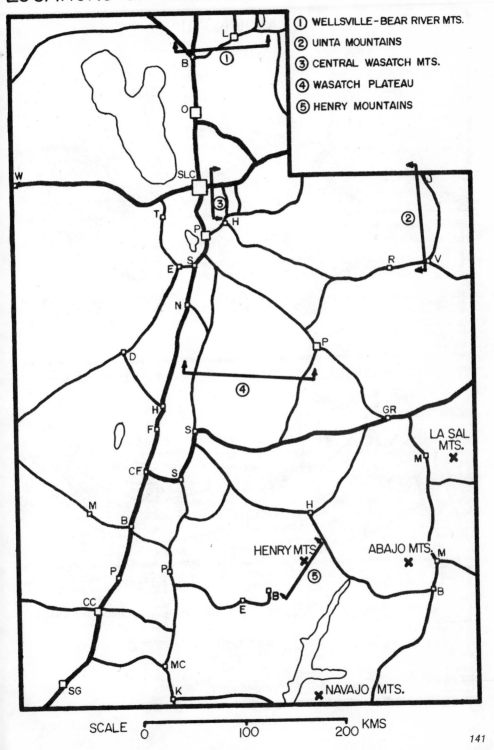

① WELLSVILLE - BEAR RIVER MTS.
② UINTA MOUNTAINS
③ CENTRAL WASATCH MTS.
④ WASATCH PLATEAU
⑤ HENRY MOUNTAINS

SCALE 0   100   200 KMS

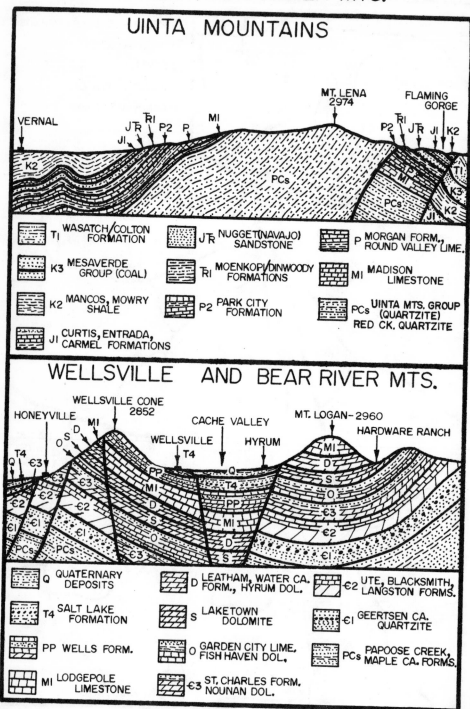

UINTA MOUNTAINS

Tl	WASATCH/COLTON FORMATION	JꝨ	NUGGET(NAVAJO) SANDSTONE	P	MORGAN FORM., ROUND VALLEY LIME.
K3	MESAVERDE GROUP (COAL)	Ꝩl	MOENKOPI/DINWOODY FORMATIONS	Ml	MADISON LIMESTONE
K2	MANCOS, MOWRY SHALE	P2	PARK CITY FORMATION	PCs	UINTA MTS. GROUP (QUARTZITE) RED CK. QUARTZITE
Jl	CURTIS, ENTRADA, CARMEL FORMATIONS				

WELLSVILLE AND BEAR RIVER MTS.

Q	QUATERNARY DEPOSITS	D	LEATHAM, WATER CA. FORM., HYRUM DOL.	€2	UTE, BLACKSMITH, LANGSTON FORMS.
T4	SALT LAKE FORMATION	S	LAKETOWN DOLOMITE	€1	GEERTSEN CA. QUARTZITE
PP	WELLS FORM.	O	GARDEN CITY LIME, FISH HAVEN DOL.	PCs	PAPOOSE CREEK, MAPLE CA. FORMS.
Ml	LODGEPOLE LIMESTONE	€3	ST. CHARLES FORM, NOUNAN DOL.		

CENTRAL WASATCH MTS.- NORTH

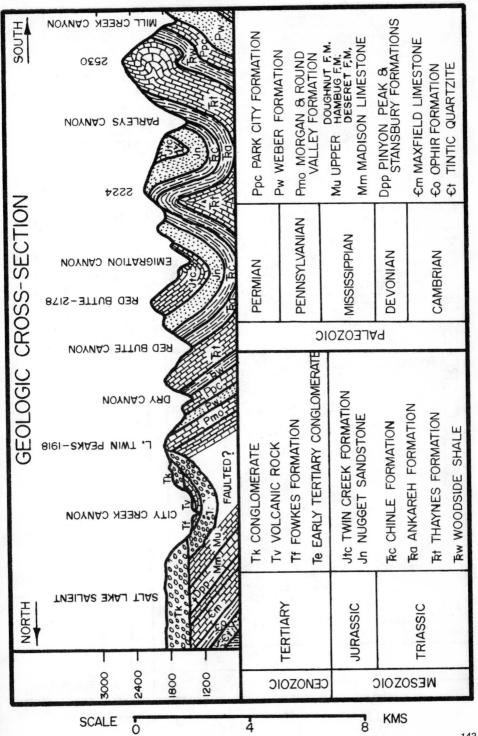

GEOLOGIC CROSS-SECTION

CENOZOIC	**TERTIARY**	Tk CONGLOMERATE Tv VOLCANIC ROCK Tf FOWKES FORMATION Te EARLY TERTIARY CONGLOMERATE		
MESOZOIC	**JURASSIC**	Jtc TWIN CREEK FORMATION Jn NUGGET SANDSTONE		
	TRIASSIC	℞c CHINLE FORMATION ℞a ANKAREH FORMATION ℞t THAYNES FORMATION ℞w WOODSIDE SHALE		
PALEOZOIC	**PERMIAN**	Ppc PARK CITY FORMATION Pw WEBER FORMATION		
	PENNSYLVANIAN	Pmo MORGAN & ROUND VALLEY FORMATION		
	MISSISSIPPIAN	Mu UPPER	DOUGHNUT F.M. HAMBUG F.M. DESERET F.M.	
		Mm MADISON LIMESTONE		
	DEVONIAN	Dpp PINYON PEAK & STANSBURY FORMATIONS		
	CAMBRIAN	€m MAXFIELD LIMESTONE €o OPHIR FORMATION €t TINTIC QUARTZITE		

SCALE 0 — 4 — 8 KMS

SOUTH

MILL CREEK CANYON
2530
PARLEYS CANYON
2224
EMIGRATION CANYON
RED BUTTE–2178
RED BUTTE CANYON
DRY CANYON
L. TWIN PEAKS–1918
CITY CREEK CANYON
SALT LAKE SALIENT
NORTH

FAULTED?

3000
2400
1800
1200

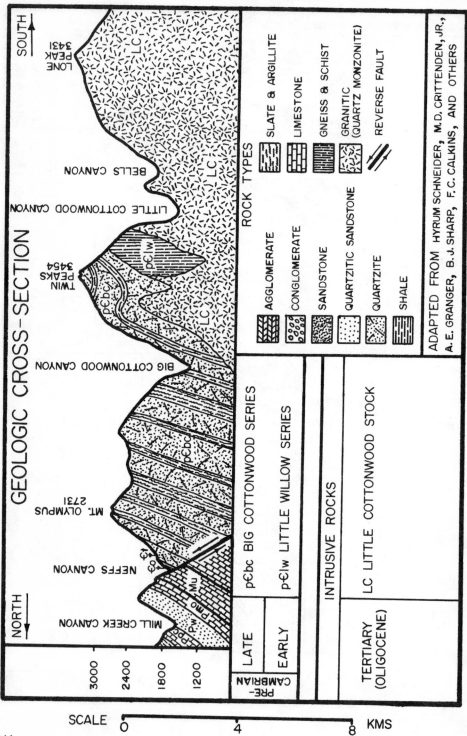

CENTRAL WASATCH MTS.–SOUTH

GEOLOGIC CROSS-SECTION

SOUTH

LONE PEAK 3431

LC

BELLS CANYON

LITTLE COTTONWOOD CANYON

LC

TWIN PEAKS 3454

pЄbc

pЄlw

LC

BIG COTTONWOOD CANYON

pЄbc

MT. OLYMPUS 2731

NEFFS CANYON

Mu

Pw

Pmo

MILL CREEK CANYON

NORTH

3000
2400
1800
1200

ROCK TYPES

SLATE & ARGILLITE	
LIMESTONE	
GNEISS & SCHIST	
GRANITIC (QUARTZ MONZONITE)	
REVERSE FAULT	

AGGLOMERATE	
CONGLOMERATE	
SANDSTONE	
QUARTZITIC SANDSTONE	
QUARTZITE	
SHALE	

LATE	pЄbc BIG COTTONWOOD SERIES	
EARLY	pЄlw LITTLE WILLOW SERIES	
PRE-CAMBRIAN	INTRUSIVE ROCKS	LC LITTLE COTTONWOOD STOCK
	TERTIARY (OLIGOCENE)	

ADAPTED FROM HYRUM SCHNEIDER, M.D. CRITTENDEN, JR., A.E. GRANGER, B.J. SHARP, F.C. CALKINS, AND OTHERS

SCALE 0   4   8   KMS

144

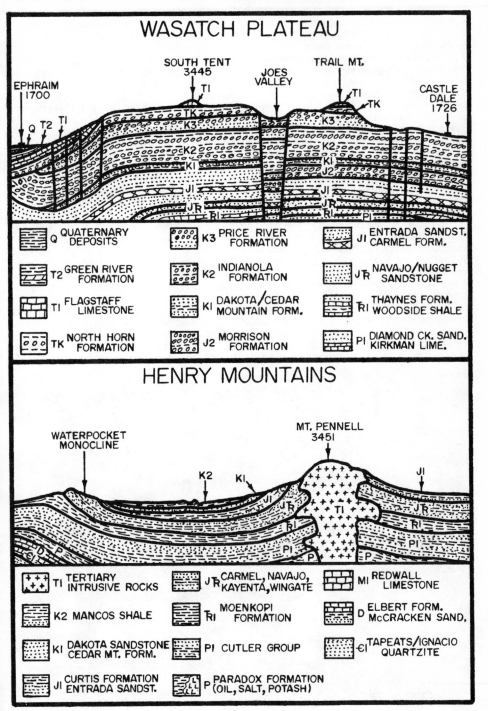

WASATCH PLATEAU

SOUTH TENT 3445
JOES VALLEY
TRAIL MT.
EPHRAIM 1700
CASTLE DALE 1726

	Q	QUATERNARY DEPOSITS		K3	PRICE RIVER FORMATION		JI	ENTRADA SANDST. CARMEL FORM.
	T2	GREEN RIVER FORMATION		K2	INDIANOLA FORMATION		JR	NAVAJO/NUGGET SANDSTONE
	TI	FLAGSTAFF LIMESTONE		KI	DAKOTA/CEDAR MOUNTAIN FORM.		RI	THAYNES FORM. WOODSIDE SHALE
	TK	NORTH HORN FORMATION		J2	MORRISON FORMATION		PI	DIAMOND CK. SAND. KIRKMAN LIME.

HENRY MOUNTAINS

WATERPOCKET MONOCLINE
MT. PENNELL 3451
K2
KI
JI

	TI	TERTIARY INTRUSIVE ROCKS		JR	CARMEL, NAVAJO, KAYENTA, WINGATE		MI	REDWALL LIMESTONE
	K2	MANCOS SHALE		RI	MOENKOPI FORMATION		D	ELBERT FORM. McCRACKEN SAND.
	KI	DAKOTA SANDSTONE CEDAR MT. FORM.		PI	CUTLER GROUP		€I	TAPEATS/IGNACIO QUARTZITE
	JI	CURTIS FORMATION ENTRADA SANDST.		P	PARADOX FORMATION (OIL, SALT, POTASH)			

Utahs Anasazi and Fremont Indians

In southeastern Utah canyons, many of which are included in this book, are found many archaeological ruins, and petroglyphs and pictographys, left behind by what now is known as the Anasazi and Fremont Indians. The following is an excerpt adapted from the information on the BLM publication, "Grand Gulch Primitive Area" (map).

[The Basketmakers were the earliest known inhabitants of Grand Gulch. This culture is thought to have derived from an earlier nomadic people whose livelihood was based on hunting and gathering. As yet no artifacts have been discovered in the Gulch which pre-date the Basketmakers. When the nomadic people learned to plant and cultivate corn introduced from the south (as well as squash and beans and the domestication of turkeys), they became more sedentary and the Basketmaker culture evolved. It flourished here from 200 to 600 A.D. They built pit houses made of mud, caked over stick walls and roofs. Their name was derived from the finely woven baskets they made. They also used flint tools and wooden digging sticks. The most prevalent remains of the Basketmaker culture in the Gulch are their slab-lined storage cists. These may still be seen on the mesa tops or on high ledges protected from the weather (and rodents).

A series of droughts apparently drove the people into the surrounding mountains. When they returned around 1050 A.D., their culture had been influenced by the Mesa Verde people to the east and the Kayenta people from the south. As time passed the Mesa Verde influence predominated in the Grand Gulch Area.

The Basketmaker culture had developed into the Pueblo culture. The Pueblo culture is characterized by the making of fine pottery with some highly decorated; the cultivation of cotton and weaving of cotton cloth, and the high degree of architectural and stone masonry skill seen in the cliff dwellings in the Gulch. They also developed irrigation of their crops by building checkdams and diversion canals. These have been found on the mesa tops near Dark Canyon and tributary canyons to the Colorado River. The kiva, a round ceremonial structure found in Grand Gulch, is still in use by the modern day descendants of the Anasazi, the Hopi and New Mexico Pueblo Indians.

Grand Gulch is also known for the diversity of rock art scattered throughout. The rock art consists of both petroglyphs (pecked into the rock) and pictographs (painted on with pigments). As the figures do not represent a written language, the meaning of the various panels is left to our imaginations.

Periods of drought in the 12th and 13th centuries, plus depletion of natural resources and pressure from nomadic Indians from the north, are thought to be some possible reasons for the abandonment of

A close-up of Newspaper Rock, located on the paved highway running to The Needles.

UTAHS ANASAZI AND FREMONT INDIANS

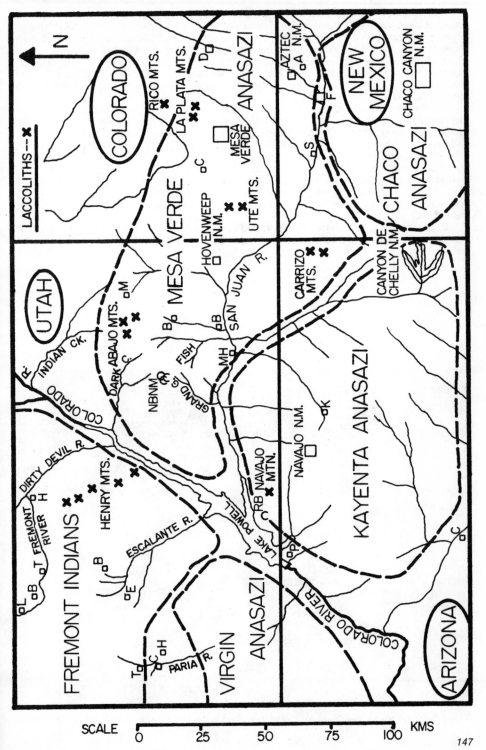

this region. By the late 1300's, the Anasazi moved south into Arizona and southeast into the Rio Grande Valley of New Mexico.]

Places where Anasazi ruins can be found are in Grand Gulch, Fish and Owl Creeks, Dark Canyon, Natural Bridges National Monument, and in various other canyons not covered in this book. The map shows the general boundaries of the Mesa Verde Anasazi, to which Utahs Anasazi belonged. It also shows the land areas occupied by other groups of Anasazi during the same time period, namely the Virgin, Kayenta and the Chaco Anasazi. It also shows part of the land covered by the Fremont Indians. Evidence of the Fremonts is found in the Escalante River drainage, in Capital Reef National Park and the Fremont River system in that same area. View their rock art on panels at Newspaper Rock and in the Fremont River Gorge.

The Fremonts were people who lived in this area during the same time period as the Anasazi. The main populations of Fremonts apparently lived in Castle Valley (southwest of Price) and in Nine Mile Canyon. They ranged from Utahs high plateaus, to the Uinta Mountains, south to the Escalante River, and east into Colorado. They hunted and fished, and grew corn, squash and beans, using some primitive irrigation ditches. But they differed from the Anasazi in these ways: They built less durable homes in the river bottoms or on ridges, but not under cliffs. They used animal skins to make moccasins, instead of using sandals as worn by the Anasazi. They depended on hunting much more than their cousins to the southeast. They didn't grow or use cotton, or raise turkeys. And the ceremonial kiva was apparently never used or developed. It appears the Colorado River was a cultural and physical impediment.

Evidence shows the Fremont culture thrived from about 950 A.D. until 1250 or 1300 A.D. It's thought they too were driven out by drought. It's also thought that they remained in the same general area and their descendants are now the Utes and Southern Piutes.

Grand Gulch granaries, reached only by ladders. Food is dry and away from rodents (105mm lens).

Foto shows vandalized kiva at Junction Ruins, in the Grand Gulch (17mm lens).

These are vandalized pictographs seen on the road to the San Rafael Campgrounds (105mm lens).

Utah Maps and Dealers

The Utah Travel Council publishes a series of 8 maps covering the state of Utah. These maps are 1:250,000 scale, and have contour lines. These maps are especially good for areas not covered by the national forest maps, and for areas in the Great Basin and the southeastern part of the state. Because of the intermediate scale, they bridge the gap between state highway and forest service or U.S.G.S. maps. These can be purchased at all the national park visitor centers, many of the other outlets listed below, and at the Utah Travel Council Office, 300 North Main Street, Salt Lake City, Utah.

The U.S. Forest Service maps can normally be purchased at any of the forest service offices or ranger stations. The Intermountain Regional Forest Headquarters in Ogden has all forest service maps for the state and intermountain area. Forest service maps are especially good for the Uinta Mountains, because they show lakes. Sign posts on trails normally point the way to lakes, not mountains. Forest service maps are also good when it comes to showing access roads, and whether they are maintained or not.

Bureau of Land Management (BLM) maps can be purchased at any of their offices throughout the state, but these are often inferior to other maps.

At the time of publication of this book, most but not all, of the new metric — 1 : 100,000 scale maps have been completed. Both the U.S.G.S. and the BLM make their own series of this map, but the U.S.G.S. ones are normally better because they're one color and are much less confusing and easier to read. There are some problems with these maps, but none too serious. Some 4WD roads don't show up clearly, some 4WD roads have been eliminated, and they fail to show many man-made features. But they do cover larger areas than the 1 : 24,000 scale maps, thus one map can be bought instead of 3 or 4. A good feature about these maps is they are metric. The USA is now in the beginning stages of changing over to the metric system; making these maps is part of that first step. Sooner or later we will all have to make the change. If one is now beginning a collection of maps, these metrics are recommended. The author has visited 100 countries in his 13 years of travel, and can count on one hand the number of countries that still cling to the old English system of measurement. The sales and distribution of this book may suffer some because it's metric, but in the end, all authors will have to change and revise their books — except this one.

Dealers for Topographic Maps In Utah

(USGS maps 1 : 250,000, 1 : 100,000 (Metric), 1 : 62,500, and 1 : 24,000 scale, and national parks and monuments of various scales)

Arches National Park
Visitor Center
Brian Head
Brian Head Nordic Ski Center
Bryce Canyon National Park
Visitor Center
Canyonlands National Park
Needles Visitor Center
Capital Reef National Park
Visitor Center
Cedar City
Mountain View Real Estate
110 North, Main

Cedar Breaks N.M.
Federal Building
Cedar Breaks National Monument
Visitor Center
Delta
Portraits Forever Studio
242 East, Main
Duchesne
Jerry D. Allred and Associates
121 North, Center
Green River
Ken Sleight Expeditions
16 North, Long St.

Kanab
Utah Properties, Inc.
30 West, Center

Wilderness Sports
240 South, 100 East
Logan
Trailhead Sports
35 West, 100 North
Moab
Arches National Park HQ.
Canyonlands National Park HQ.
Bridges National Monument HQ.
446 South, Main

The Times Independent
35 East, Center

Tourist Information Center
North Highway
Ogden
Great Basin Engineering, Inc.
3505 Grant Ave.

Weber State College Bookstore
3750 Harrison Blvd.
Park City
Timberhaus Ski & Sports
628 Park Ave.

NDEX MAP FOR 1:100,000-SCALE METRIC MAPS

GROUSE CREEK	TREMONTON	LOGAN		
NEW FOUNDLAND MOUNTAINS	PROMONTORY POINT	OGDEN		
BONNEVILLE SALT FLATS	TOOELE	SALT LAKE CITY	KINGS PEAK	DUTCH JOHN
WILD CAT MOUNTAIN	RUSH VALLEY	PROVO	DUCHESNE	VERNAL
FISH SPRINGS	LYNNDYL	NEPHI	PRICE	SEEP RIDGE
TULE VALLEY	DELTA	MANTI	HUNTINGTON	WEST WATER
WAH WAH MTS. NORTH	RICHFIELD	SALINA	SAN RAFAEL DESERT	MOAB
WAH WAH MTS. SOUTH	BEAVER	LOA	HANKSVILLE	LA SAL
CEDAR CITY	PANGUITCH	ESCALANTE	HITE CROSSING	BLANDING
ST. GEORGE	KANAB	SMOKEY MTN.	NAVAJO MTN.	BLUFF

TOPOGRAPHIC MAPS PRINTED AND DISTRIBUTED BY THE U.S. GEOLOGICAL SURVEY (INTERMEDIATE SCALE)

SCALE 0 100 200 KMS

Provo
Utah Office Supply Co.
69 East Center Street
Salt Lake City
Federal Building (USGS)
25 South State

Holubar Mountaineering
3975 Wasatch Blvd.

Intermountain Aerial Surveys
2078 West 2300 South

Kirkham's Outdoor Products
3125 South State

Photo-Blue
370 South, West Temple

Sunset Sports Center
1110 East 7200 South

Timberline Sports, Inc.
3155 Highland Drive

Wasatch Mountain Touring
779 East, Third South
Snowbird
Timberhaus Ski & Sport
Snowbird Village
Springdale
Zion National Historical Assn.
St. George
Spoke and Pedal
90 South, 100 East
Timpanogos Cave National Mon.
Visitor Center
Torrey
Boulder Mountain Realty

Bushnell Real Estate, Inc.
Vernal
Bitter Creek Books
672 West, Main
Zion National Park
Visitor Center

US Geological Survey Sales Offices

All USGS Topographic maps may be purchased over the counter or by mail order from:

Branch of Distribution
U.S. Geological Survey
Federal Center
Denver, Colorado

A limited stock of the standard topographic quadrangle maps is maintained for over-the-counter sales only at:

1012 Federal Building
1961 Stout Street
Denver, Colorado

1036 General Service Building
19th & F Streets N.W.
Washington, D.C.

Public Inquiries Office
USGS National Center, Room 1C402
12201 Sunrise Valley Drive
Reston, Virginia

Map Reference Libraries In Utah

Cedar City
Library, Southern Utah State College
Logan
Library, Utah State University
Ogden
Library, Weber State College
Provo
Library, Brigham Young University
Salt Lake City
Library, University of Utah
Salt Lake City Public Library

Surrounding States

Tucson Arizona
Summit Hut, 4044 East Speedway
Boise, Idaho
Jenson-graves Co., 210 North, Eight Street
Baker, Nevada
Lehman Caves, National History Association
Las Vegas, Nevada
Causey Engineering Service, Ltd., 1000 East Charleston Boulevard
Mercury Blueprint & Supply Co., 1425 South Main Street
Albuquerque, New Mexico
Holman's, 401 Wyoming Blvd., N.E.
Farmington, New Mexico
San Juan Reproduction Co., 135 N. Airport Drive

U.S. Forest Service Offices and Ranger Stations

ASHLEY NATIONAL FOREST
Headquarters
437 East Main
Vernal, Utah

Duchesne Ranger District
85 West Main Street
Duchesne, Utah

Flaming Gorge Ranger District
Dutch John Unit
P.O. Box 157
Dutch John, Utah

Green River Unit
1540 Uinta Drive
Green River, Wyoming

Manila Unit
Manila, Utah

Roosevelt Ranger District
150 South 2nd East
Roosevelt, Utah

Vernal Ranger District
650 North Vernal Avenue
Vernal, Utah

DIXIE NATIONAL FOREST
Headquarters
82 North 100 East
Cedar City, Utah

Cedar City Ranger District
82 North 100 East
Cedar City, Utah

Enterprise Ranger Station
Enterprise, Utah

Escalante Ranger District
Escalante, Utah

Pine Valley Ranger District
196 East, Tabernacle Street
St. George, Utah

POWELL RANGER DISTRICT
225 East Center
Panguitch, Utah

Teasdale Ranger District
Teasdale, Utah

FISHLAKE NATIONAL FOREST
Headquarters
170 North Main Street
Richfield, Utah

Beaver Ranger District
190 North 100 East
Beaver, Utah

Castle Dale Ranger Station
Castle Dale, Utah

Ephraim Ranger Station
Ephraim, Utah

Ferron Ranger Station
Ferron, Utah

Fillmore Ranger District
390 South Main
Fillmore, Utah

Loa Ranger District
150 South Main
Loa, Utah

Manti Ranger Station
Manti, Utah

Monticello Ranger Station
Monticello, Utah

Mt. Pleasant Ranger Station
Mt. Pleasant, Utah

Richfield Ranger District
55 South 100 East
Richfield, Utah

SAWTOOTH NATIONAL FOREST
Headquarters
1525 Addison Avenue East
Twin Falls, Idaho

UINTA NATIONAL FOREST
Headquarters
88 West 100 North
Provo, Utah

Heber Ranger District
125 East 100 North
Heber City, Utah

Nephi Ranger Station
Nephi, Utah

Pleasant Grove Ranger District
390 North 100 East
Pleasant Grove, Utah

Spanish Fork Ranger District
44 West 400 North
Spanish Fork, Utah

WASATCH NATIONAL FOREST
Headquarters
8226 Federal Building
125 South State Street
Salt Lake City, Utah

Evanston Ranger District
Federal Building
221 10th Street
Evanston, Wyoming

Kamas Ranger District
50 East Center Street
Kamas Utah

Logan Ranger District
910 South Highway 89-91
Logan, Utah

Mountain View Ranger District
Lone Tree Road, Highway 44
Mountain View, Wyoming

Ogden Ranger District
Federal Building
324 25th Street
Ogden, Utah

Salt Lake Ranger District
6944 South 3000 East
Salt Lake City, Utah

Bureau Of Land Management (BLM)
Offices And Ranger Stations

BLM UTAH HEADQUARTERS
University Club Building
136 East, South Temple
Salt Lake City, Utah

CEDAR CITY DISTRICT
Headquarters
1579 North Main Street
Cedar City, Utah

Beaver River Resource Area
44 South Main
Cedar City, Utah

Dixie Resource Area
24 East, St. George Blvd.
St. George, Utah

Escalante Resource Area
Escalante, Utah

Kanab Resource Area
320 North First East
Kanab, Utah

MOAB DISTRICT
Headquarters
125 West, 2nd South Main
Moab, Utah

Grand Resource Area
Sand Flats Road
Moab, Utah

Price River Resource Area
900 North, 7th East
Price, Utah

San Juan Resource Area
284 South, 1st West
Monticello, Utah

San Rafael Resource Area
900 North, 7th East
Price, Utah

RICHFIELD DISTRICT
Headquarters
150 East, 900 North
Richfield, Utah

Henry Mountain Resource Area
Hanksville, Utah

House Range Resource Area
Fillmore, Utah

Sevier River Resource Area
180 North, 100 East
Richfield, Utah

Warm Springs Resource Area
Fillmore, Utah

SALT LAKE DISTRICT
Headquarters
2370 South 2300 West
Salt Lake City, Utah

Bear River Resource Area
2370 South 2300 West
Salt Lake City, Utah

Pony Express Resource Area
2370 South 2300 West
Salt Lake City, Utah

VERNAL DISTRICT
Headquarters
170 South 500 East
Vernal, Utah

Bookcliffs Resource Area
170 South 500 East
Vernal, Utah

Diamond Mtn. Resource Area
170 South 500 East
Vernal, Utah

National Parks and Monuments of Utah
(HEADQUARTERS OFFICES)

Arches National Park
446 South Main Street
Moab, Utah

Bryce Canyon National Park
Bryce Canyon, Utah

Canyonlands National Park
446 South Main Street
Moab, Utah

Capital Reef National Park
Torrey, Utah

Cedar Breaks National Monument
82 North, 100 East
Cedar City, Utah

Dinosaur National Monument
Dinosaur, Utah

Glen Canyon National
Recreation Area
Page, Arizona

Natural Bridges National Monument
446 South, Main Street
Moab, Utah

Rainbow Bridge National Monument
Page, Arizona

Zion National Park
Springdale, Utah

This foto shows two of several spires making up the Fisher Towers near Moab (35mm lens).

Further Reading

History

Canyon Country Prehistoric Indians, Barnes and Pendleton, Wasatch Publishers, Inc., 4647 Idlewild Road, Salt Lake City, Utah.

Incredible Passage (Through the Hole-in-the-Rock), Lee Reay, Meadow Lane Publications, Provo, Utah.

Canyon Country Geology, F.A. Barnes, Wasatch Publishers, Inc., 4647 Idlewild Road, Salt Lake City, Utah.

Guide Books

Canyon Country Hiking, Fran. A. Barnes, Wasatch Publishers, Inc., 4647 Idlewild Road, Salt Lake City, Utah.

Capitol Reef National Park — A Guide to the Roads and Trails, Ward J. Roylance, Wasatch Publishers, Inc., 4647 Idlewild Road, Salt Lake City, Utah.

Guide to the Trails of Zion National Park, Zion Natural History Association, Springdale, Utah.

High Uinta Trails, Mel Davis, Wasatch Publishers, 4647 Idlewild Road, Salt Lake City, Utah.

Hikers Guide to Utah, Dave Hall, Falcon Press Publishing Co., Inc., Billings and Helena, Montana.

Wasatch Trails — Volume I, Betty Bottcher, Wasatch Mountain Club, Salt Lake City, Utah.

Wasatch Trails — Volume II, Daniel Geery, Wasatch Mountain Club, Salt Lake City, Utah.

Other Books by the Author

Climbers and Hikers Guide to the Worlds Mountains, Michael R. Kelsey, Kelsey Publishing, 310 E. 950 S., Springville, Utah, USA.

Orderville Canyon, a tributary to Zion (Narrows) Canyon, is one of the narrowest (35mm lens).

From the top of the Hole-in-the-Rock. One can see Lake Powell far below (17mm lens).

Typical scene in Coyote Gulch. A deep, dark, cool, well-watered canyon (50mm lens).

INDEX

Mt. Nebo as seen from Mona. North peak left, south peak right (35mm lens).

With good weather, winter climbs on Timp can have a happy ending at the summit. (50mm lens).